Corner
Conversations

Corner
Conversations

Engaging Dialogues About God and Life

Randy Newman

Corner Conversations: Engaging Dialogues About God and Life

© 2006 by Randy Newman

Published by Kregel Publications, a division of Kregel, Inc., P.O. Box 2607, Grand Rapids, MI 49501.

Library of Congress Cataloging-in-Publication Data
Newman, Randy.
Corner conversations: engaging dialogues about God and life / by Randy Newman.
    p. cm.
1. Apologetics. 2. Witness bearing (Christianity). I. Title.
BT1103.N49   2006
239—dc22   2006007065

ISBN 0-8254-3323-1

Printed in the United States of America

06 07 08 09 10 / 5 4 3 2 1

This book is lovingly dedicated to Pam,
my lifelong conversation partner.

Contents

Acknowledgments

MOST PEOPLE SKIP THE ACKNOWLEDGMENTS PAGE, but I hope you won't. No one travels a spiritual journey alone, and I'm no exception. It may be that hearing about my fellow travelers will encourage you as you take your next steps.

The idea for this book was developed on a long car ride with my son Jon during the summer of 2003. Jon and I drove from Virginia to Colorado and back, spent a summer in a "bachelor apartment," and enjoyed many dinners of macaroni and cheese. Jon's honest questions along with his forthright critiques of superficial answers challenged me to write this series of dialogues.

My desire has been to help people find answers for themselves. Good friends listened to my ideas, offered suggestions, or read portions of my manuscript. They helped make it a better work. For their honest critiques, I am indebted to Karen Alexander, Josiah Case, Dave Fossum, Greg Ganssle, Bruce and Cathy Graves, Lin Johnson, Derrick Lovick, Anders Lundegard, David McGaw, Janet Merritt, J. P. Moreland, Tim Muehlhoff, Josh Owens, Bob Ragan, Becky Slack, Mike Summers, and J. D. Weiman.

I'm especially grateful to Don Carson for his insight and help, and to Jim Weaver and all the friends at Kregel for their wisdom and expertise.

During the writing of this book, some difficult times visited my family. As a result, the topics I was addressing in *Corner Conversations*—God, suffering, meaning in life, and so forth—took on deeper significance and urgency. During those trying days, several close friends encouraged me to keep writing despite the setbacks. Without the "lifelines" from Spencer and Barbara Brand, Patrick and Karey Dennis, Frank and Judy Kifer, David Case, Don Knox, and Mark Petersburg, I might have quit. Pam and I also found great support from the listening ears and heartfelt prayers of our house-church friends Paul and Sue Cowan, Corky and Georgie Eddins, Charlie and Esther Powell, and Jeff and Vicki Thornhill.

I'm grateful to my parents, Marty and Rhoda Newman, for staying committed to each other for more than fifty years. You don't know what strength that gives me!

To all my family, Pam, Dan, David, and Jon—thank you for loving me enough to listen to me even when I repeat myself, to laugh at my jokes even when they're not funny, and to let me know when I'm taking myself too seriously.

Jon, I hope you like this product of that great summer we had together.

Introduction

WELCOME TO TURNERVILLE. I ONLY WISH THIS town existed someplace besides in my imagination. Everything moves slowly in Turnerville. People take time to think. They discuss issues that typically get rushed or ignored. Even the leaves seem to change colors more slowly there. When city planners drew up blueprints, they strategically placed benches all over town so people would stop and chat. The mayor boasts of a higher bench-per-capita ratio than any other locale.

Don't you long for that kind of community? Don't you hunger for relaxed conversations instead of anxious fly-by messages? I do. In a day when most conversations take place through e-mail, instant messaging, or on cell phones with intermittent reception ("Can you hear me now?"), taking time just to listen and interact seems luxurious.

It also sounds scary. Such a level of intimacy requires vulnerability, reflection, and humility. But I say it's worth the risk.

I also long for conversations with people who disagree with me—conversations, not arguments. Do these still exist anywhere? When I turn on the television and catch one of those so-called "talk" shows, I hear something other than talk. I'm assaulted by people yelling at and interrupting each other. I cringe as participants make sarcastic cracks about points their opponents really aren't making. I observe simultaneous monologues instead of respectful dialogues. Such noise makes me thankful for that great technological wonder—the remote control.

Don't you sometimes wish you could express doubts without someone jumping down your throat? Wouldn't it be helpful to have friends who correct you (gently!) when you say something foolish, but also let you formulate thoughts without condemning you? Wouldn't it be nice to speculate and then, once you've heard something come out of your mouth, have the freedom to say, "Oh, wait a minute. I don't really believe that"? And wouldn't it be great to have people listen to your uncertainty and just say, "Oh, that's okay"?

People in Turnerville give each other that kind of liberty. I dream that such conversations will become more the norm—for real and not just in my imagination. And in what area do we need this kind of freedom and respect more than in religion and spirituality? We live in a more pluralistic and diverse age than ever but we sound more intolerant and fearful than ever.

In the midst of this tense atmosphere, *Corner Conversations* addresses difficult and complex topics:

- Can we really know God?
- Why does God allow evil and suffering?
- Aren't all religions basically the same?
- Should we believe the Bible?
- Whose morality is best?
- Why are there so many hypocrites among believers?
- Is there life after death?

How often are subjects like these addressed in healthy, robust exchanges? How common are the commodities of careful listening and reflection? It's my hope that we can change a disturbing pattern and promote respect without compromise, convictions without arrogance, and listening without patronizing.

Before you start eavesdropping on the residents of Turnerville, let me explain a few things.

The conversations written in this book aren't real—but they are realistic. I didn't transcribe them from actual tape-recorded chats. But after working on college campuses for the past twenty-five years, sharing many a cup of coffee with students and professors, I can assure you these kinds of exchanges between people of differing perspectives do take place.

Corner Conversations is also drawn from situations besides the university campus. Sideline chats at soccer games, exchanges with neighbors and relatives, and question-and-answer sessions with my sons (and some of their peers) have provided plenty of fodder for what you find on these pages.

You should know, too, that I'm a follower of Jesus. Everyone has some bias. Mine favors what Christians have traditionally believed for the past two thousand years. I try to focus my life around the core beliefs that all Christians affirm—what C. S. Lewis called "mere Christianity."

At the same time, I value fairness and respect. I've tried to model those virtues in the conversations I've created and have sought even-handedness. Several friends with contrary viewpoints read my work to see if I was erecting straw men. They assured me I represented them fairly.

I value healthy exchange between people of different faiths. I grew up in a Jewish home in a Catholic neighborhood, went to public schools, and came to follow Jesus as the promised Messiah at Temple University, a diverse urban university. That decision came after years of debate— with others, within my own mind, and with consultation of two thousand years' worth of dialogue between two different yet connected worldviews.

I'm comfortable with the process of holding these differing values in healthy tension, but I also press for conclusions. Regarding process, I realize this book is only one of many steps on your spiritual journey. I hope it won't be the last thing you read about Jesus, his teaching, his work, and God's plan for your life. After each conversation you'll find a section of endnotes suggesting further reading, Web sites to visit, and parts of the Bible to investigate. If you have to choose only one additional read, I hope you'll choose the biblical section.

This love for process might frustrate you. I ask more questions than I answer. Some of these dialogues leave issues unsettled. I'm okay with that, but I thought it best to warn you.

On the other hand, I put a premium on landing the plane, not just enjoying the flight. Years ago, I saw a sign outside a professor's office that intrigued me. It said, "Better to debate an issue without settling it than to settle an issue without debating it." I guess. But I wonder if we have other alternatives. How about settling an issue after debating it? Many people today pride themselves for searching without ever finding. I think we'd all, deep down, rather search and find.

Here's one more preference that has shaped this book. I hate interruptions. So I didn't want to flood the pages with footnotes. I didn't even want those little numbers luring you toward the back of the book. Instead, the sections of endnotes, entitled "Keep the Conversation Going," give credit where credit is due, along with references to page numbers and key words.

Sorting out religious beliefs can be taxing—intellectually, emotionally, and spiritually. But can you think of anything more important, more foundational, or more influential in shaping who you will become? You've picked up this book because you have some level of interest in clarifying or expanding your beliefs. Maybe a good friend gave or lent it to you with the hope that you two will engage in some lively conversations and enhance your friendship. Wouldn't that be great?

For whatever reasons you've arrived at this point, I'm grateful for the opportunity to join you in your quest for answers and insight. Maybe someday we could sit on a bench somewhere and chat about it. I'd like that.

In the Hospital Parking Lot

Wrestling with Evil and Suffering

CATHY DAVIDSON TAKES HER JOB TOO SERIOUSLY, or so her friends tell her. Having just begun her fifteenth year at Turnerville Memorial Hospital, she's considered a seasoned veteran by her colleagues. But her interactions with dying patients always take an emotional toll on her. Even during nursing school, when working on the relatively joyful maternity ward, Cathy spent many evenings in tears on the bus ride home. Whenever a premature baby struggled to survive or complications prevented new mothers and fathers from celebrating in the usual ways, Cathy struggled more than most of her classmates. Now she specializes in oncology and the tears flow almost daily.

Many of her nurse colleagues develop a detached professionalism; others simply don't spend a lot of time thinking about the difficult issues of life. But Cathy can't seem to apply either solution. More than most people, she wrestles with questions like, "How could a good God allow such evil and suffering?" None of the answers she's heard so far have satisfied her.

Her longtime friend and colleague, Janet Walsh, shares her depth of concern for these questions but somehow finds answers. Janet's religion gives her a sense of stability that Cathy finds appealing yet elusive.

Living near each other, they commute on the same bus, carpool to the same soccer practices, and yell at the same swim meets. Over the years, they've become good friends. Although Cathy attended church as a child, once the pressures of work and motherhood filled her schedule, church dropped by the wayside. Janet has a similar background but has always made her faith a priority. She had attended Nurses' Christian Fellowship throughout college and even served as an advisor for a chapter at Turnerville High.

The bus stop bench at the southwest corner of the hospital parking lot provides a location for many a conversation about pain. There, hospital workers and visitors wait for their transport to home. On this particular Thursday, Janet and Cathy engage in the first of two such exchanges on that bench. A second conversation—by two other hospital workers, in the same location, on the same topic, with a very different tone—will take place hours later.

❖

CATHY:	Ladies and gentlemen, mark your calendars! Janet and Cathy arrive early to work—that's a first. We've got a whole thirty minutes before our shift starts. Let's sit outside here on this bench until we have to go in.
JANET:	Yeah, it's a beautiful day.
CATHY:	I'm amazed I even came back to work at all today, after yesterday's horrors.
JANET:	Why? What happened?
CATHY:	Oh . . . that's right. You weren't here yesterday. Where were you?
JANET:	I had to meet with Jimmy's philosophy teacher. Why they try to teach philosophy to high school kids is beyond me. I wish they'd just wait and let them struggle with the meaning of the universe until after they've gone away to college. Then I wouldn't have to deal with Jimmy's questions about Kant and Hume and a bunch of German names I can't pronounce.
CATHY:	I could use an appointment with a philosopher.
JANET:	Why? What's going on?

CATHY: Mr. Freidman finally died last night.
JANET: Oh.
CATHY: But it gets worse. That young girl . . . Amber. She also
            left us.
JANET: No! What happened? She was doing so well. We
            thought she beat her cancer.
CATHY: To be honest, Janet, I really don't know. That's the
            thing about this oncology unit. There's no rhyme
            or reason to the outcomes. Some people come in
            here and go home healthy. Some go to the morgue.
            Sometimes the chemo works. Sometimes it doesn't.
            But even in a good week we have a pretty low success
            rate. We deal with death all the time. What I wouldn't
            do to work maternity again, like back in nursing
            school.
JANET: We've been at this for a long time, Cathy.
CATHY: I know. But I really think it's taking a bigger toll on
            me than I expected.
JANET: I know what you mean. That's really terrible about
            Amber. How are her parents taking it?
CATHY: They freaked out. It was terrible. Sue and Terry tried
            to comfort them but they just couldn't stop crying.
JANET: They must be devastated. She was making such good
            progress.
CATHY: I'm really serious, Janet. I don't know how much more
            of this I can take. I really need to get some answers.
            I don't mean any disrespect, but how can you hang
            on to your faith when, all day long, you see such
            suffering and death?
JANET: I don't know how I'd make it any other way.
CATHY: You've told me that before. I just don't get it. What do
            you know that I don't? Why does your God let people
            suffer so much?
JANET: You think I know the answer to that?
CATHY: Don't you?

JANET:	No. I've got some tiny pieces to the puzzle. But I wouldn't claim to have it all figured out. Cathy, I come home sometimes and wrestle with the exact same questions you do.
CATHY:	Really?
JANET:	Really.
CATHY:	Well, do you mind if I ask you about these kinds of things?
JANET:	No. I wish more people would. I think it's good to wrestle with questions like why God allows suffering. I just don't think we'll get it all figured out—this side of heaven, anyway.
CATHY:	Or in the next twenty minutes before going back to work.
JANET:	Actually, it's probably best to take this question in twenty-minute chunks. Much more than that at a time makes my head hurt.
CATHY:	Me too. But let's start. What did you mean by "pieces of the puzzle"?
JANET:	I think we've got *some* answers. But none of them totally answers the whole question of suffering or evil.
CATHY:	So . . . you're saying that if you add all the pieces up, that makes a complete answer?
JANET:	Ha! Don't I wish. No. I think if you add up all these pieces, you still have a big part of the question unanswered. It's almost like we've got slivers of a pie chart. But even after you label a bunch of the slivers, you've still got this big slice of pie with a question mark on it.
CATHY:	And what *are* some of these slivers you're talking about?
JANET:	I guess the biggest one is the whole thing about free will.
CATHY:	That God made people with the ability to choose?
JANET:	Yes. Although it's more than just choosing—like

whether to have regular or decaf. It's the freedom to choose whether we follow God or reject him.

CATHY: Isn't this like some kind of big debate between Christians? Don't some Christians think we're just robots and God preordains everything?

JANET: This sounds like the appointment I had with Jimmy's philosophy teacher yesterday. Cathy, I'm even less of a theologian than a philosopher. But here's what I do understand about that controversy. I don't think any Christian thinks we're just robots. But anybody who claims to understand the whole free-will-versus-God's-will thing is claiming to know more than the Bible tells us. In some places, when there's a discussion about this in the Bible, it uses words like *unfathomable* or *unreachable*. So I don't think we can fathom the unfathomable.

CATHY: That's frustrating.

JANET: Maybe. Maybe not. But let's come back to that. I do think, though, that we have *some* amount of free will, and that explains a whole lot of suffering. Like the people who check into the floor below us—where Jodie and Lisa work in detox. All those drug problems are caused by people making their own terrible choices—to put drugs into their bodies.

CATHY: All of them? How about those little babies? They were born addicted to crack because their mothers smoked it while they were pregnant. That's not the baby's fault!

JANET: I know . . . and I go home in tears whenever I hear about that. That's why I call these things slivers—they don't explain *everything*. They just help with some of the story.

CATHY: I guess.

JANET: The thing about free will that *I* just recently realized is that, in some way, it's a really amazing display of

	God's love for us. He didn't want us to be robots. So he gave us some freedom. That's the essence of being a person—instead of a bench!
CATHY:	Even if it means that some people choose evil?
JANET:	I'm afraid so. But love, if it's not freely given, isn't love it all. Instead, it would be like some guy saying, "I love you," only because you're pointing a gun to his head. That's not love.
CATHY:	That's for sure.
JANET:	Another sliver is the whole Adam and Eve thing. Christians call it *the fall* but that sounds too passive. It was more like a rebellion.
CATHY:	You mean when they ate the apple? What's that got to do with our oncology ward?
JANET:	The point of that story is that they both chose to do what they wanted to do instead of obeying God. The Bible says, as a result of that rebellion, the whole world is out of whack.
CATHY:	Where does it say that?
JANET:	Right there at the end of the story, in the first book of the Bible—Genesis. In chapter 3. It shows how, when Adam and Eve disobeyed God, it messed up their relationship with each other, with God, and even with the world around them. And we're still dealing with the aftereffects. In the New Testament, in Romans, it says that "the whole creation groans" as a result.
CATHY:	So . . . that's the Christian explanation for earthquakes and tidal waves and stuff like that?
JANET:	Again, it's just a partial explanation.
CATHY:	Okay. This is helpful. I'm surprised you haven't mentioned the Devil. Isn't he responsible for all the suffering in the world?
JANET:	All? That's hard to say. Laying a percentage of blame here or there is tough when it comes to the question

of evil and suffering. In a sense, yes, I guess the Devil is behind all the evil in the world. The Bible does say that he's much more evil than we think. He was jealous of God so he kind of led a rebellion and God punished him for it. He's still trying to make God look bad.

CATHY· Why?

JANET: We're getting out of my league here, Cathy. I remember some stuff I once learned in a Sunday school class, but if you really want to learn about this, I could bring you some things to read.

CATHY: No thanks. I don't really want to concentrate on the Devil. I don't think I would've gone to a whole Sunday school class about Satan.

JANET: It wasn't *all* about Satan. It was about a whole set of basic Christian beliefs. I think it's important to know some things about the Devil, though, even though people make fun of the whole notion.

CATHY: I know I *used* to—until I saw that character in the Mel Gibson movie, *The Passion*. That guy was creepy.

JANET: You know, I thought the way they portrayed the Devil in that movie was really good. He or she—it was kind of hard to tell; it wasn't quite human—was just attractive enough to draw you in but just repulsive enough that you wanted to gag.

CATHY: Exactly.

JANET: Well, that's kind of how the Devil is. He's really seductive, and he tempts people to want to be their own god—just like he did to Adam and Eve. But then he comes through with his real agenda—and it's always evil and death or destruction.

CATHY: So he's kind of the mastermind behind all the suffering in the world.

JANET: Again, I don't know about percentage on this.

CATHY: But God is more powerful than the Devil—isn't he?

JANET: Yes, he certainly is. Just read the beginning of the
            book of Job; you'll see that the Devil can do only what
            God lets him do—no more. God's more powerful.

CATHY: What God lets him do!? Why does God let him do
            anything?

JANET: I don't know. That's the unanswered part of this
            question.

CATHY: I'll say. You tell me that God is powerful. Can he do
            anything?

JANET: Yes.

CATHY: Okay. He's all-powerful. And you say he's good.

JANET: Right.

CATHY: So he could stop evil if he wanted to. And he should
            want to because he's good.

JANET: Right.

CATHY: So why *is* there evil?

JANET: You've just stated the problem better than any
            philosopher.

CATHY: Thanks. But I'm still really frustrated.

JANET: I know. I've got a few more insights about this but,
            to be honest, I don't think it'll totally relieve the
            frustration. You have a lot of questions about God,
            and my beliefs have a *lot* of answers, and the answers
            I do know have a lot of good in them. I think they
            outweigh the unanswered questions. And I believe
            there *are* satisfying answers to all of our questions. It's
            just that we're not going to get all of those answers in
            this life.

CATHY: So you live with some mystery.

JANET: I have to.

CATHY: Well . . . I still don't like your partial answers.

JANET: They're a lot better than the alternatives.

CATHY: What do you mean?

JANET: There are just a bunch of *wrong* answers to this
            question. My incomplete answers may be difficult

	to live with, but they're better than all those wrong answers. And they're not only wrong, they're just too easy.
CATHY:	Like what are some of these "easy" answers?
JANET:	Like atheism, for example. It's an easy answer to the problem of suffering, but it's so arrogant for someone to say, "I know there is no god."
CATHY:	I'm not an atheist. I think there's way too much evidence for some kind of supernatural force behind the universe. And I think there's something inside of us that cries out for some kind of god. So I agree with you there. Atheism's too easy.
JANET:	I think reincarnation's probably the easiest answer. But I don't buy it.
CATHY:	Why do you say it's the easiest?
JANET:	Because people who believe in reincarnation see suffering as a result of something they did in a past life.
CATHY:	That *is* kind of hard to argue with.
JANET:	You'd have to travel back in a time machine to prove them wrong.
CATHY:	So maybe they're right.
JANET:	I doubt it. But I'm basing my disbelief in reincarnation on my belief in Jesus' resurrection.
CATHY:	Okay. I think we've gotten off the point. You don't have to convince me that reincarnation's a bad answer for suffering. It doesn't solve the problem any more than the Christian answer. And in a sense, it just makes things worse. If I believed that acting bad in a past life caused suffering , I'd be frustrated by evil. And I'd also feel guilty that I caused it, or I'd get mad at someone else, thinking they're the cause of evil. That just doesn't seem right or even fair.
JANET:	I'm glad you see that.
CATHY:	I feel like we're not making any progress, though.

JANET: Well, we're ruling out some bad explanations. That's
            progress.

CATHY: Atheism's too simple. Reincarnation's too
            condemning. What else do you have?

JANET: The worst wrong answer, I think, is a really popular
            one. It's the one that says that God just can't help it. He
            can't stop evil because he's just not powerful enough.

CATHY: People really believe that?

JANET: You ever hear of the book, *When Bad Things Happen
            to Good People*?

CATHY: Of course. I read it.

JANET: That's what the rabbi who wrote that book claims.

CATHY: He's a rabbi and he believes that?

JANET: And people love his book!

CATHY: I know. Lots of people bring it up to the hospital and
            give it to patients.

JANET: I can understand why it's such a best seller. The
            rabbi's a really great writer.

CATHY: And very compassionate. Didn't his son die from
            some terrible disease?

JANET: Progeria.

CATHY: I can't imagine what that must've been like.

JANET: Me either. So he's very warm and comforting. But his
            bottom line is that God just couldn't stop the disease,
            and that there are just some things that even God
            can't do.

CATHY: I remember feeling really uncomfortable when I got
            to the end of his book. Didn't he say that we had to
            forgive God for his shortcomings?

JANET: Yes.

CATHY: Why is he still a rabbi? Why would anyone want to
            worship such a wimpy god?

JANET: Cathy, you're brilliant. You should think about
            teaching Jimmy's philosophy class. You make tons
            more sense than his teacher.

CATHY:	If people keep dying on our floor, I might consider a job change.
JANET:	Listen, your response to Harold Kushner's book is right. If God is so weak, our world is in a lot of trouble—more than if he's the kind of God the Bible says he is. *When Bad Things Happen to Good People* is a terrible book because it concludes the exact opposite of the book of Job. Even when some of Job's biggest questions were unanswered, he still said, "I know God can do all things."
CATHY:	I guess I have to confess my ignorance. You keep mentioning Job. I've never read it. Can you give me the CliffNotes version?
JANET:	I'm sorry . . . I just assumed you'd read it, but I shouldn't have.
CATHY:	No problem.
JANET:	So, you want the CliffNotes version. That's not the best way to find out about Job, but here goes. There was this guy named Job who had it all—wife, lots of kids, lots of land, money, you name it. This all took place a long time ago—even before Abraham.
CATHY:	Okay.
JANET:	One more thing. Job's really a good man. A righteous man. God even says he's an upright and blameless man.
CATHY:	Wow. God said that?
JANET:	Yeah. So the Devil goes to God one day and says, "The only reason Job loves you and is a righteous man is because you make life easy for him. Anybody would love you if they were in Job's place." So the Devil makes this bet with God: if everything were taken away from Job, he'd curse God.
CATHY:	And God goes for that?
JANET:	Yes. Big time.
CATHY:	I thought you said this was a good book. I haven't even read it and I hate it already.

JANET: I used to hate it too. Now I love it.

CATHY: Why?

JANET: I'll tell you after I finish the CliffNotes and the Janet notes.

CATHY: I can hardly wait for the Janet notes.

JANET: So the Devil takes everything away from Job—well, almost everything. His house, his possessions, and even his children—all killed in one fell swoop.

CATHY: Gross.

JANET: And Job still praises God.

CATHY: So the Devil loses the bet.

JANET: Round one, at least. The Devil comes back to God and asks to strike Job's health.

CATHY: And God lets him?

JANET: Yep. And still Job praises God. Although his wife tells him he's nuts.

CATHY: How come God didn't take away his wife?

JANET: Good question. Considering how she responded, maybe it was tougher for Job with her still around!

CATHY: Ha! Is there some kind of happy ending after all this?

JANET: Yes, but I've only told you the first two chapters.

CATHY: How long is this book?

JANET: Forty-two chapters. And it's only in the last chapter that God returns some things to Job. In fact, it says that the second part of Job's life was more prosperous than the first. And he had more kids too.

CATHY: And I suppose people think that made all the suffering worthwhile?

JANET: I don't think that's the way people take it. If they do, it's a pretty shallow view of suffering.

CATHY: So what happens in between chapters 3 and 42? That's a lot of space you skipped.

JANET: I know. That's why I wasn't happy about giving you just the CliffNotes version. In between, there's really not a lot of action but there's a whole lot of dialogue

	between Job and his friends, and then between Job and God.
CATHY:	Dialogue! It'd better be riveting.
JANET:	Actually, it is—once you get into it. Like I said, at first I hated the book of Job. It was just so frustrating because after all this dialogue between Job and his friends, there's the climax of the book—God shows up and dialogues with Job.
CATHY:	And tells him why he put him through all that garbage, right?
JANET:	You would hope so. But he doesn't!
CATHY:	And yet you like this book? Why?
JANET:	I don't know if I can answer that unless first you read it for yourself. All those dialogues are told in poetic language. It's actually kind of therapeutic to read.
CATHY:	But it never answers the question of why God allowed the Devil to do all that to Job.
JANET:	I know. But you should see the way God talks to Job at the end. At first it almost seems cruel. He asks Job a million questions—just like Job had been asking him. He asks Job if he was there when God created the world, if he knew how the world worked, if he understood all the mysteries of nature and stuff like that.
CATHY:	So what does Job say?
JANET:	At first nothing. He puts his hand over his mouth.
CATHY:	I don't get this.
JANET:	Then he confesses that he was wrong for claiming to understand more than he really did. It's as if he realized that God is the one who's in charge of the universe, not Job. And if God wants to run his world in a way that doesn't always make sense to Job, that's his business.
CATHY:	So you're saying that Job doesn't get an answer but that's okay with him?

JANET: Yes . . . in a sense. God put him in his place and Job accepted that. I think the message of Job is a very humbling one. It tells us that we need to give up our demand for God to explain himself to us.

CATHY: Because he's not going to.

JANET: Exactly. So we're left with a choice. Do we demand an answer that we're not going to get? Or do we let God be God and worship him, even though there are things about him we don't understand?

CATHY: That's really hard.

JANET: Only until you give up seeing yourself as the one in charge. When you realize you're not—that God does things beyond our understanding, and he doesn't need to explain it to us—it's actually liberating.

CATHY: But couldn't God tell us why he does things the way he does?

JANET: He could—but I'm not sure it would do us any good.

CATHY: Of course it would.

JANET: I'm not so sure. Lots of kids come into the hospital here and have to get some pretty painful procedures. They always yell, "Why!" But that's not what they really need at that moment. A kid just needs her mom or dad to hold her and tell her it's okay. If some really smart doctor sat down with a kid and explained all the reasons why there had to be pain to bring about healing, the kid wouldn't want to hear it.

CATHY: And it wouldn't make the whole experience any less painful.

JANET: Right.

CATHY: Are you saying, then, that we go through suffering because it'll bring us some kind of healing?

JANET: Sometimes. I think that's another one of those slivers.

CATHY: Like what kind of healing do Amber's parents get after losing her to cancer?

JANET: Okay. I'm going to answer your question—but it's

only speculation on my part. I can't get into someone else's head and know what they're experiencing. But I don't want you to dismiss my answer as simplistic. There really is something to this—but you've got to think about it.

CATHY: Okay. I won't just dismiss it.

JANET: There are some kinds of really difficult lessons in life that we can only learn through really difficult means. I believe there's such a thing as eternity, and God made us for eternity, not for just this temporary world.

CATHY: You mean heaven?

JANET: Yes. In fact, if there's no such thing as eternity, then all the suffering in the world is totally absurd. If I didn't believe in God and eternity and heaven, I'd go insane after seeing all the suffering we see in the hospital.

CATHY: You *do* have a point here. Mr. Freidman's family is really religious, and they seemed to have a more peaceful way of handling his death than most other families I see.

JANET: You're right. Mr. Freidman became a Christian soon after he was diagnosed. The rest of his family had been Christian for a while and had been praying for him. So they had a way to see his suffering that gave it some meaning—even if it wasn't all the meaning they might hope for.

CATHY: You should've seen it, Janet. It was like watching two different movies overlapping each other. One was about this horrible death he was dying and the other was about how peaceful he was.

JANET: I can believe it.

CATHY: And then, right before he took his last breath, he sat up straight in his bed and looked off into space, with his eyes really wide and said, "Wow!" It was almost like he saw God.

JANET: Why do you say, "almost"?

CATHY: Hmm.

JANET: Here's what I'm trying to say. Mr. Freidman, you, me, and everyone else are made for heaven, not just our time on earth. But he didn't realize that before he got cancer so he was living just for this life. It took cancer to get his attention so he'd be ready for the next life.

CATHY: So God uses suffering to wake us up out of our delusion and get us ready for heaven?

JANET: I think so. I've read stories about people who've gone through hard things, and they say it's made them more sensitive, or more caring, or more focused on God than on themselves.

CATHY: Or it makes them more bitter!

JANET: Yeah. But there's that choice thing again. God still gives us the ability to look at our circumstances, and we decide if we'll be thankful or bitter. One author said, "The same sun softens the butter or hardens the clay."

CATHY: Hmm. More for me to think about. I just don't feel like that's all there is to it, though. God brings bad stuff into our lives to prepare us for heaven or teach us to not be so selfish?

JANET: I never said that's *all* there is to it.

CATHY: You're right. You did make that clear. This is just a whole different way to think about this. It's going to take a little time for me to sort it out in my head.

JANET: I know. But I need to add one more point to all this. We've left out an important part of the picture.

CATHY: What's that?

JANET: Jesus. Like I said, I have to see all this in light of eternity and God. The fullest picture we have of eternity and God is Jesus, his death on the cross, and his resurrection.

CATHY: But he's not mentioned in the book of Job.

JANET: Actually, he is. Well, not by name. But Job realized
            that all his suffering, and all that God was doing,
            would someday make a lot more sense when his
            Redeemer—that's what he called him—would stand
            on the earth and put all this into perspective.

CATHY: He was like a prophet, then, foretelling the future?

JANET: Yes. And if he could put his suffering into perspective,
            seeing his Redeemer off in the distant future—then
            we really shouldn't leave Jesus out of the picture if
            we're tying to make sense out of suffering.

CATHY: Making sense out of suffering—I like the way you put
            that.

JANET: Thanks, but I didn't think it up myself. It's the title
            of a really good book by a man named Peter Kreeft. I
            wish people brought *that* book to patients instead of
            When Bad Things Happen to Good People. I got it as
            a gift from Mr. Freidman when he first checked into
            the hospital. He said it was the only book that helped
            him—other than the Bible.

CATHY: Should I read that before or after I read Job?

JANET: After.

CATHY: Okay. But—yikes! Look what time it is. We need
            to get to work—otherwise, really bad things might
            happen to two really good people—us!

JANET: Ha!

CATHY: But I'd like to continue this conversation. Do you
            have any lunch plans?

JANET: Nope.

CATHY: Okay. Then more Job at noon. Let's go.

❖

Later that day, in the hospital cafeteria.

❖

JANET:	Is today going any better than yesterday?
CATHY:	I think so. Nobody's died yet. But it turns out that I have to eat and run. I have to get back.
JANET:	No problem. Well, I've had a better day. I haven't had to deal with any philosophy teachers.
CATHY:	Great. You know, after our discussion this morning, I really got to thinking about what you said.
JANET:	About what specifically?
CATHY:	When you said that suffering is really absurd if there's no god or no heaven. Well, you know Michael, the anesthesiologist?
JANET:	Tall guy?
CATHY:	Yeah. Well, he's an atheist and he's always making snide comments about religion. He's really pretty nasty.
JANET:	Don't tell me . . . you invited him to lunch.
CATHY:	No. I need a nice lunch. But I did ask him something.
JANET:	Uh-oh.
CATHY:	No, it was good. I asked him how he, as an atheist, makes sense out of Mr. Freidman's passing or Amber's.
JANET:	Good for you. What'd he say?
CATHY:	Actually he kind of got pretty mad at me. He didn't really answer the question and just said something like, "The existence of evil and suffering proves there's no god."
JANET:	Proves? That's a pretty bold statement!
CATHY:	But you know, Janet, it's not that I think evil proves that God doesn't exist. My question isn't about his existence. It's about his goodness. These philosophical types, like Michael, don't get my point. They want to debate the existence of God, and they say that the existence of evil wins the debate for the atheists. But I don't think it does.
JANET:	I think you're right. Like I said this morning,

atheism's too simple of an answer, given the complexity of life.

CATHY: I agree. But I'm still stuck on why we should worship this God or follow him. I don't mean to sound crude, Janet, but I almost want to say, "What's God's problem that he demands that people worship him?" If some guy ever said that, you'd think he was so conceited that he was pathetic.

JANET: That's a different question than the one we were discussing this morning. Did Michael bring this up?

CATHY: No, Michael just got mad at me for asking him a question he couldn't answer. If there's no god, what's the atheistic explanation for evil—and he didn't have an answer. So I'm with you. I like your partial answer better than his non-answer.

JANET: Good. I'd rather have you on my side than on Michael's.

CATHY: But what do you say to my question? Why does God have such a big ego?

JANET: Mmm. I never thought about that. Give me a minute.

CATHY: Sure. Do you understand what I'm asking?

JANET: Yeah. But I'm wondering if your question assumes something about God that isn't really true.

CATHY: Like what?

JANET: That he's like us, maybe?

CATHY: What do you mean?

JANET: Why do you think God shouldn't demand worship?

CATHY: Because it's conceited.

JANET: And what's so bad about being conceited?

CATHY: Are you serious? When people are conceited, it's because they think they're better than they really are.

JANET: People. Yes. But does God think he's better than he really is?

CATHY: I'm not sure.

JANET: I don't see how God *could* think that. He's perfect.

He's pure goodness and pure holiness. There's no one or no thing that's better than he is. So he can't be conceited. It's a category that just doesn't fit who he is.

CATHY: Now I'm *really* glad Michael didn't join us for lunch.

JANET: Do you see my point, Cathy?

CATHY: I think so.

JANET: The problem is—and it's all related to this issue of evil and suffering—is that we think in the wrong categories. Maybe there's something more to life than just pleasure and being happy all the time. Maybe there's something about responding to death and disease in a heavenly way that's better than just asking *why* all the time. And maybe God is so much bigger and better than anything we can imagine, that he's worthy of our worship.

CATHY: I've really got to think about this. But I like your way of talking about it better than how some skeptics do. And I'm still wrestling with the way Mr. Freidman's family handled his cancer and his death better than almost any other family that's been up here.

JANET: It almost says more about God than it does about them.

CATHY: I don't follow.

JANET: The way Christians handle suffering. People always marvel at them and wonder how they can be so accepting of bad circumstances and how they can have such great faith. But maybe all that says more about what a great God they trust rather than anything about themselves.

CATHY: This great God you keep talking about—couldn't he have just made a world with no evil or suffering to begin with?

JANET: He did!

CATHY: Oh. Yeah. That free will thing again. Okay. But why doesn't he do something about evil now?

JANET: Two answers—he has and he will.

CATHY: Two responses—I eat and you explain.

JANET: He *has* done something about evil. He sent his Son
            to die to pay for it. Do you remember when I talked
            about that verse in Genesis 3—the one about the
            whole world being out of whack as a result of Adam
            and Eve's rebellion?

CATHY: Yeah, I remember.

JANET: Well, it also predicts Christ's death. It says that an
            offspring from the woman will have conflict with the
            Devil, but he'll win. The Bible is more poetic than
            that, but that's the gist of it.

CATHY: Okay.

JANET: So God *has* done something about evil. He died to
            pay for it. And people who trust in that death have a
            way of handling evil and suffering that really ticks off
            the Devil. The Devil lost the battle with the Messiah
            and he keeps getting reminded of it every time
            someone handles death or sickness with a Christian
            perspective.

CATHY: But evil still does some really terrible things. Why
            hasn't God gotten rid of it totally?

JANET: Yet! He hasn't gotten rid of it yet! He will.

CATHY: How can you be so sure?

JANET: Because of what he's already done to evil. Jesus'
            resurrection was the shattering blow to evil. It was so
            climactic that it gives me confidence that the rest of
            the solution is on its way.

CATHY: You know, I really want to believe what you believe.
            I'm just not there yet. You don't have all the answers,
            but you're not stupid either.

JANET: Well, thank you very much!

CATHY: I'm sorry. That didn't come out the way I meant it.

JANET: Now it's my turn to eat while you explain.

CATHY: I know. Now I sound like the stupid one.

JANET: No you don't. You're trying to process some pretty
            difficult stuff. It took me years.

CATHY: What I mean is that you don't claim to have it all
            figured out, but you don't just stick your head in the
            sand and stop thinking.

JANET: Ah. Thanks.

CATHY: And if there's one thing you've made me think about,
            it's that I need to look at this whole question of evil in
            a different way—like from a larger perspective. I've
            got to consider that God is bigger than I think and
            that Jesus' death is part of this picture.

JANET: You got it!

CATHY: Let's keep talking.

JANET: And don't forget to keep reading.

CATHY: Job?

JANET: Yeah. But I'd also suggest one of the Gospels—
            probably John's. That'll help keep the perspective
            right.

CATHY: I'll do that. But not now. I've got to get back to work.
            Are you taking the bus home?

JANET: Yup—like always.

CATHY: I'll see you then.

❖

At 5:10 that afternoon, sitting on the same bench where Cathy
and Janet began their conversation, Michael and Tom resume their
ongoing debate about God.

Michael chose anesthesiology because it was the crossroads of many
medical specialties. He needed expertise in pediatrics, gerontology,
and every stage in between. He enjoyed the challenge of teaming
with cardiologists, oncologists, neurologists, and obstetricians, and
working with patients of almost every age and with a wide variety
of ailments. But he sometimes wondered if he chose anesthesiology
from a lack of desire to "settle down," medically speaking, or from a
true love for the whole spectrum of human life.

More at the core of Michael's soul is a deep-seated harshness. Just ask anyone around him. A master of sarcasm, he commandeers many a conversation with his barbs against religion, God, or anyone who takes their faith seriously. He especially enjoys posing questions that stump his Christian colleagues. Almost as if he has a checklist, he takes pride in the fact that most of the religious people who had once "tried to convert him" now simply keep their distance.

Except Tom. An MD, specializing in oncology, Tom will sometimes respond to Michael's attacks in ways that sound, to some bystanders, almost as caustic as the ones from the skeptic. But in a strange way, Michael respects his coworker for that very reason. He mixes it up and challenges Michael in ways that no one else ever has.

Tom found Christian faith later in life than many people. After four years of relatively easy undergraduate study (a combination, he would often quip, of "wine, women, and occasional biology classes"), he hit the wall of academic challenge during his first year of med school. Nothing had ever defeated him the way that first year of classes had, and it became a crisis of all kinds of belief—in himself, in his career, and in his God—although he'd be hard pressed to tell you which god he was doubting.

The summer after that difficult year—a time of wondering whether he should go back to the world of microscopes and white coats—Tom started attending church. He came to understand what a personal relationship with God could look like. By the time he returned for that crucial second year of med school, he had a new faith, a new perspective on life, and a new determination to excel in the medical profession.

But that's another story and one that now has ten years of history after it. For the past year, Michael and Tom have been debating faith in a way that challenges both of them. Their dialogues, like the one recounted below, stimulate both of them—but annoy just about anyone who overhears. Long ago, they agreed to cease fire as soon as other people arrived within shouting distance.

(If you find this kind of arguing difficult to hear, you might want to skip the rest of this chapter. Then again, sometimes a good argument can shed light on an otherwise unexamined topic.)

❖

MICHAEL: Well, another day, another dollar—and, of course,
            another death. Mr. Freidman finally kicked the bucket.

TOM: You have such warmth and compassion. I'll bet your
            patients feel so comforted by your great bedside manner.

MICHAEL: Most of my patients have their backs to me as I stick
            needles into their spines. And before long, they're
            sound asleep, so my bedside manner means nothing
            to them.

TOM: That's a relief.

MICHAEL: You have to admit. Mr. Freidman's family was a pain
            to listen to, with all their singing and crying.

TOM: Oh, come on. They were watching a loved one die.
            Have you no heart at all? I think it was great the way
            they handled his passing. I hope I have that kind of
            chorus around me as I leave this world.

MICHAEL: I'm sure it helped Mr. Freidman feel a bit more
            peaceful. I'll be honest with you, Tom. I really wish
            I could have that kind of faith—like the way you
            believe in God or the way that old man did.

TOM: Really? You? Mr. I-eat-Christians-for-breakfast
            Skeptic?

MICHAEL: I'm not that bad.

TOM: Sure you are. Just ask all the Christians you've cursed
            out in the past year.

MICHAEL: I haven't cursed out anyone.

TOM: Sarah Serling?

MICHAEL: Okay. But she deserved it.

TOM: Because she told you she was going to pray for you?
            Michael, *I* can take some of your harshness but that
            doesn't mean it's okay to talk that way to everyone.

MICHAEL: But I just have so much fun poking holes in your
            religion.

TOM: But you just said you wish you could believe what we
            did. How's that fit?

MICHAEL:	I wish I could believe. Really. You seem to have a lot of answers and you seem to have found some kind of peace. I just can't buy all the stuff you believe in order to get that peace.
TOM:	Why not?
MICHAEL:	'Cause it's ridiculous. People rising from the dead, God speaking in some guy's ear so he could write the Bible. I just don't buy any of it.
TOM:	Then why do you say you wish you could believe what we believe? Do you mean you wish you could be stupid like us?
MICHAEL:	I never called you stupid.
TOM:	You said that what we believe is ridiculous. What would you call a person who believes something that's ridiculous? Stupid? Insane? Retarded? Which derogatory term are you using today?
MICHAEL:	I'm not calling you any names. I just can't see how you believe some of the stuff you do.
TOM:	Fine. Just don't give me the patronizing line of "I wish I could believe what you believe" if you don't really mean it.
MICHAEL:	I didn't mean any offense.
TOM:	Okay, so which ridiculous belief would you like to discuss today—before our bus comes and we change topics and talk about the weather or the Mets.
MICHAEL:	The Yankees! Rooting for the Mets is proof that you *are* stupid after all.
TOM:	Okay. We'll stick to talking about the weather, once we get on the bus.
MICHAEL:	Good. The topic before the bus comes is suffering. You saw Mr. Freidman last night. He's a guy who prays to God every day for healing. His family sings songs about Jesus all day long. The guy's a good father, good husband, nice guy, pays his taxes, you name it—and still this God of yours doesn't answer his prayers and he dies. Why?

Tom: First of all, don't say God didn't answer his prayers.
              He did. Just not with the answer you would've liked.
              God's answer was: "No. I won't heal you. I'll take you
              home to heaven. And I'll be the source of comfort and
              hope for your grieving family."

Michael: Well, thank you very much, Mr. God.

Tom: You call yourself an atheist—right?

Michael: Yeah.

Tom: So what's your atheistic answer for Mr. Freidman's
              suffering?

Michael: What?

Tom: C'mon, Mike. Everyone, atheist or Christian or
              whatever, needs to find some way to explain the
              suffering they see. What's your explanation for why
              Mr. Freidman suffered?

Michael: I haven't really given it a lot of thought.

Tom: You've got to be kidding me! You mean you spend
              all your time poking fun at people who have a faith
              answer, but you have no opinion on the subject?

Michael: Yes, I do have an opinion. But you won't like it very
              much.

Tom: Try me.

Michael: Because stuff happens, that's why.

Tom: How very sophisticated of you. That's your answer
              for why there's leukemia or AIDS or why terrorists
              blow themselves up around the world? Because stuff
              happens? Does that really satisfy you?

Michael: Not really, but I try not to think about it too much. It
              doesn't do any good to dwell on it.

Tom: But you do dwell on it, Michael. Every one of your
              attacks toward a Christian has the subtext of trying to
              figure this out.

Michael: Says who?

Tom: Says your tone of voice and the fact that you can't
              pass by a single opportunity to talk about your

	faith. You're one of the biggest religious fanatics I know!

TOM: *(continued)* faith. You're one of the biggest religious fanatics I know!

MICHAEL: Bull. I'm not religious at all. I told you—I'm an atheist.

TOM: Then why are you talking about God all the time?

MICHAEL: I don't know what you're talking about.

TOM: Sure you do. You just don't like it when people give you the same grief you dish out.

MICHAEL: I've never seen you so worked up, Tom.

TOM: Good. That's two of us—two religious fanatics at the bus stop.

MICHAEL: Back to the topic. Do you have a better answer than mine?

TOM: You mean your brilliant "stuff happens" explanation?

MICHAEL: Yeah.

TOM: Yes. I do have a better answer—it's just not a complete one.

MICHAEL: What do you mean?

TOM: I mean there's plenty about suffering and evil that I don't understand. And I don't ever expect to. But my faith helps me find hope and meaning in the midst of suffering. And it's a whole heck of a lot better than despair or sarcasm or your brand of harsh criticism.

MICHAEL: Now who's doing the attacking?

TOM: You're right. I'll back off. But if you're really serious about hearing my answers, I think you'll find that there's some substance to them. They give me a sense of stability in a pretty unstable world—especially the world of oncology where I hang out.

MICHAEL: That's saying something. You do see a lot of people die.

TOM: And not without a toll on me. I get pretty down sometimes. But without my faith in Christ, I'd jump off a bridge somewhere. My trust in things like Jesus' suffering gives me the confidence that other people's suffering isn't pointless.

MICHAEL: Well, I don't know about all that.

TOM: Do you want to?

MICHAEL: Huh?

TOM: Do you want to know? Do you even want to consider
            the fact that there might be something to all this?
            Or do you just want to blab your opinion at people?
            Which is it, Mike? Do you want truth or just a place
            to air your attacks?

MICHAEL: Wow. Listen, you need to take a chill pill and get off
            your high horse. I did give God a try once. I asked
            for answers and he kept his mouth shut. I looked to
            him for some kind of answer to a prayer and he didn't
            answer—or, excuse me, he gave me the answer, "No."
            Same result.

TOM: When was this?

MICHAEL: When my mother died. Ovarian cancer. It really
            sucked.

TOM: I didn't know about that. I'm sorry.

MICHAEL: It was before I started working here.

TOM: Ah.

MICHAEL: Anyway, your wonderful God didn't show up. I went
            looking for him, and he played hide-and-seek. So I
            said, "Later." He can go play that game with other
            people if he wants. I'm done.

TOM: Are you sure you were looking for him?

MICHAEL: What do you mean?

TOM: Were you looking for him—for God—to know him
            for who he is—or were you looking for healing for
            your mother?

MICHAEL: I was looking for God to heal my mother. I'm not
            following where you're going with this.

TOM: I'm sorry. I don't mean to be cruel. You're obviously
            upset about losing your mother. That must have been
            horrible.

MICHAEL: Yeah. And that was eight years ago. It still hurts.

TOM: I'll bet it does.

MICHAEL: But you asked if I was looking for God or for healing?
          I don't see the difference.

TOM: If you were really seeking God, you'd want to find
          him for who he really is—not just as a rabbit's foot to
          rub so your mother would get better.

MICHAEL: What's wrong with wanting my mother not to suffer
          from cancer?

TOM: Nothing. But you should be honest about it. You
          were seeking your mother's well-being or your own
          emotional relief. But you weren't seeking God.

MICHAEL: I don't see how I could have under those
          circumstances.

TOM: I'm not sure I do either.

MICHAEL: You don't?

TOM: I don't think it's impossible—but it would be really
          tough. The point is, you shouldn't give up on God
          just because he didn't heal your mother. You should
          be honest enough to admit that you weren't really
          seeking God in the first place and you should consider
          a sincere search.

MICHAEL: Huh. I think that's the first intelligent thing I've heard
          you say.

TOM: There's that old bedside charm again.

MICHAEL: Sorry. But seriously. That's worth thinking about.

TOM: Good.

MICHAEL: And here comes our bus—time for the cease-fire.

TOM: I hear it might rain tonight.

MICHAEL: Which would be a rainout for both the Yankees and
          the Mets.

TOM: That's a shame.

❖

Keep the Conversation Going

- The biblical books that can help you wrestle with the problem of evil are the book of Job and the gospel of John. Don't quit reading either book until you get to the end.
- You might also want to read

D. A. Carson, *How Long, O Lord* (Grand Rapids: Baker, 1991).

Peter Kreeft, *Making Sense Out of Suffering* (Ann Arbor: Servant, 1986).

C. S. Lewis, *The Problem of Pain* (New York: Macmillan, 1944).

Jerry L. Sittser, *A Grace Disguised* (Grand Rapids: Zondervan, 1998).

Carson's book is the most theologically deep and is primarily written for people who are already followers of Christ. Anyone can benefit from his writing but readers need to keep in mind the audience for whom the book is intended. Kreeft's book will appeal to you if you enjoy philosophy. Lewis's book is a combination of philosophy, theology, and brilliant writing. None of these are easy reads. Sittser's book tells an incredibly painful and powerful story of the author's own encounter with tragedy.

19   *unfathomable*: See Romans 11:33–36.

20   *Adam and Eve*: See Genesis 2–3.

       groan: see Romans 8:18–25.

25   *I know God can do all things*: See Job 42:2.

30   *the same sun softens the butter*: Paul Little, *Know Why You Believe* (Downers Grove, Ill.: InterVarsity, 1988), 141.

31   *Actually he is . . . Redeemer*: See Job 19:25–27.

35   *Well, it also predicts Christ's death*: See Genesis 3:15.

At The Library

*Researching if the "Good Book"
Is Any Better Than the Others*

NICK AND SUZANNE—TWO PERSONALITIES whose freshman experiences couldn't be more divergent. Good friends throughout high school, they stayed close in touch during their watershed freshman years at separate schools.

After a beer-soaked orientation week, Nick decided that college was too important to spend most of it with a hangover, as he'd done for most of high school. Getting drunk had long ago lost its luster for him. So when Nick found out that his freshman roommate didn't drink, he actually breathed a sigh of relief and decided to join him at some of the "dry" mixers he attended. It was a welcome change of pace.

Added to his new-found sobriety came an unfamiliar venture into religion. Nick's roommate, Matt, attends a Christian fellowship that distributes "Freshman Welcome Packs" outside the dining hall during the first two weeks. Nick took one from Matt simply to be polite. Most of the stuff in the pack held no appeal—except the really nice laundry bag and a copy of the New Testament, a book Nick had never read. Mid-afternoon readings from the Gospels and Romans, late-night debates with Matt over theology, and increasingly frequent attendance of a discussion series at the campus's Christian Studies Center brought Nick to the brink of conversion.

Suzanne's freshman experience could be classified on the other end of several spectrums. Raised in a Christian home, Suzanne had near-perfect attendance at her church's youth group. She brought her faith to college but figuratively stowed it near the back of her closet. Somehow the chance to "take a break" from Christianity seemed appealing. So she did.

She signed up for the Introduction to the New Testament class because the professor has a reputation as an iconoclast. He delights in challenging commonly held religious beliefs and enjoys watching students wrestle with their faith (or, as he would say, their parents's faith) for the first time in their young lives.

Suzanne found Dr. Young's classes both appealing and disturbing. Hearing someone so smart seriously look at the Bible with more than a devotional eye was enlightening. That he debunked the resurrection, the early dating of the writing, and just about every miracle recorded there, made Suzanne uneasy—but she had no idea how to refute such a smart man.

Nick and Suzanne instant messaged each other regularly. Neither has any romantic interest in the other, which gives the relationship a freedom they both appreciate. A regular dose of irony permeated their e-mails and IMs, as Nick moved closer to born-again Christian faith while Suzanne wandered further from it. Anticipating their return home in May, they arranged to meet the first Wednesday after the end of the semester at The Library, Turnerville's best sports bar, for twenty-five cent wing night. They asked for a table near the back corner, away from the bank of television screens broadcasting the day's top sporting events.

After catching up on final exams, the move back home, and ordering food, the conversation turns to the Bible—the book Nick has recently devoured and Suzanne has come to distrust.

❖

NICK: Aren't we quite the pair. You—the Christian turned skeptic—and me, the drunkard turned religious.

SUZANNE: It is funny, isn't it? But I'm not sure I'm really a skeptic. I'm just questioning a lot of stuff.

NICK: This Dr. Young guy really shook things up for you, huh?

SUZANNE: It's just that he's the first intelligent person I've ever heard talk about the Bible. I'm sorry, but now that I've heard him, I'm just bored stiff listening to our pastor or youth leader or anyone else that says they believe the Bible. If they think it's so good, why do they talk about it in such stupid ways?

NICK: I wish you could have heard Dr. Hart at the Christian Studies Center.

SUZANNE: What's he a doctor in?

NICK: History.

SUZANNE: Cool. I wish I could have heard him too.

NICK: What things bother you the most?

SUZANNE: It's a bunch of things. First of all, there are just so many crazy things in the Bible that are so hard to believe—the parting of the Red Sea, Jesus walking on water, all those healings, bringing people back from the dead. I can't believe I just accepted all those things without even thinking about them.

NICK: All right. Anything else?

SUZANNE: Don't you want to say something about miracles?

NICK: Not yet. Let me hear the whole list of problems. Although, I'm not guaranteeing I'll be able to respond to any of them. I'm just learning a lot of this for the first time myself.

SUZANNE: Right. And I don't want to mess you up. I'm glad you're finding some kind of faith. I'd never want to discourage you.

NICK: I know. Don't worry about it. What else is bothering you besides all the miraculous stuff?

SUZANNE: The whole notion that God dictated some kind of book to people seems pretty far-fetched to me. And why do we think it hasn't gotten distorted over the years, with it getting translated and passed down from generation to generation. Seems pretty simpleminded, don't you think?

NICK: *Now* I think I can say something. I used to ask the exact same questions you're asking. Isn't it possible, though, that God could have inspired a written book if he wanted to?

SUZANNE: What do you mean?

NICK: Isn't it possible, if there really is a God who created us, that he'd want us to know some things about him?

SUZANNE: Yeah.

NICK: And isn't it possible that he could make sure some things would get written down exactly the way he'd want them to?

SUZANNE: Possible? Of course. But likely? C'mon.

NICK: If he's a God who does miracles, it doesn't seem all that far-fetched to me that he'd inspire a book that's pretty unusual.

SUZANNE: It's unusual, all right. All those crazy miracles. Feeding five thousand with just a few pieces of bread and fish?

NICK: Why not? I mean, he *is* God. That's what he does for a living. You seem to have this bias against miracles. Why is that?

SUZANNE: I'm not biased.

NICK: Sure sounds like it.

SUZANNE: Well, maybe you're biased toward believing these kinds of things.

NICK: Guilty as charged. You're right. I am. At least *now* I am. I haven't always been this way. Regardless, it is a bias. I just got to the point where I had to be honest with myself and admit that I had no really good reason to be biased against the supernatural.

SUZANNE: Sure you do. You've never seen these kinds of things happen, have you? That's a good reason.

NICK: Not really. Are you saying that your experience or

	mine is the measure of all truth? Sounds pretty self-centered to me. Let me ask you this: Do you believe in dinosaurs?
SUZANNE:	What do they have to do with the Bible?
NICK:	Give me a chance. Do you believe in them?
SUZANNE:	Yes.
NICK:	Ever see one?
SUZANNE:	No.
NICK:	So you believe for some other reason than just your ability to see them.
SUZANNE:	Okay. I'll chew on that for a little bit. But what about all those stories getting passed down to us without getting exaggerated along the way. Instead of five thousand, couldn't there have been just a small group of people sharing a small amount of food, and then, over time, people expanded it to be five thousand being fed with just one boy's lunch? Maybe the real miracle was that people weren't selfish jerks, like usual, and they shared what little they had.
NICK:	Is this a suggestion from Dr. Young's class?
SUZANNE:	Yeah. He said that people must have exaggerated the story.
NICK:	And you're impressed with how intellectual he is?
SUZANNE:	That's nasty. He's really a brilliant man.
NICK:	I'm sorry. I didn't mean to be insulting. But that argument sounds pretty lame to me. It almost sounds like he's fishing for some explanation because he just doesn't want to believe the one that's in the text.
SUZANNE:	Oh, and food being multiplied doesn't sound like a stretch?
NICK:	Not for a God who can do the impossible. Either position takes some amount of assuming, Suzanne.
SUZANNE:	That's true. All right, but I still wonder if they got the reporting passed down correctly. Couldn't it be like the game of telephone? You know, where

people whisper something in the ear of the person next to them and then it goes down the line and gets distorted along the way.

NICK: I guess it could have happened that way. But it seems just as plausible that God could have made sure that it *didn't* happen. If he's the one who inspired the original writing in the first place, he could have also made sure it got copied and recopied and translated right. And by the way, there's a big difference between God "inspiring" the Bible and him "dictating" it.

SUZANNE: If we don't have the original writings, though, how do we know if it didn't get distorted along the way?

NICK: I'm no historian but Dr. Hart seemed to think that the historical evidence for it is pretty good. Think of it this way. In Washington, D.C., let's say we've got the "official yard stick" that establishes the standard for thirty-six inches. You know, in the Archives museum or someplace. Let's just suppose that in some terrorist attack, that building gets blown up and the official yard stick gets destroyed. We wouldn't have the original, but we'd have so many millions of other yard sticks that, centuries later, we could say that we do know how long an official yard is, or an official inch, or a foot and like that. You get it?

SUZANNE: So you're saying that we don't have the parchment that Matthew wrote on, but because we have so many copies, we know what he wrote?

NICK: Exactly. And there are these charts about how many manuscripts we have of the New Testament. It's pretty impressive. Have you seen what I'm talking about?

SUZANNE: Yeah, yeah, yeah. I know those charts.

NICK: C'mon. Don't sound so condescending. Did you take an intro to philosophy class this year?

SUZANNE: Yeah, so?

NICK: Did you read Plato?

SUZANNE: Yeah.

NICK: Did your professor announce at the beginning of the class, "Now, class, I want you to buy Plato's *Dialogues* and read it. But, you know, we don't have the original manuscript so we don't really know for sure what was originally written down, so maybe we shouldn't bother reading such an unreliable book."

SUZANNE: No, he didn't say that. What's your point?

NICK: What's my point? If your philosophy prof thinks it's okay to read Plato, even though we don't have the original, then the Bible is even more reliable because we've got a ton more manuscript evidence than we have for Plato. And, by the way, I think we *should* read Plato. Doesn't it bug you, though, that the Bible goes through tougher scrutiny than other books?

SUZANNE: No, because the stakes are higher.

NICK: How so?

SUZANNE: If I don't believe Plato, it's no big deal. If I don't believe the Bible, I could be going to hell.

NICK: Do you really believe that?

SUZANNE: I told you. I don't know what I believe anymore. I just wish Christians would think as deeply about the Bible as my professor does. Most of the people back at my youth group treat it like it's a fortune cookie or something.

NICK: Sorry. Is this too upsetting? Should we take a break?

SUZANNE: No, this is helpful. There weren't any people back at school I could discuss this with. How about this question? I wonder if the Bible squares with other kinds of research. Dr. Young told us about all these archeological discoveries that disproved so many places mentioned in the documents. It just makes it seem like you can't trust it.

NICK: That's interesting that he talked about archeology. Dr. Hart also talked a lot about archeology. His take on it was that more and more discoveries were lending support to trusting the Bible.

SUZANNE: I don't get it. It seems like profs can interpret archeological findings almost any way they want.

NICK: I don't think it's *any* way they want. There are some limits.

SUZANNE: That's true.

NICK: Maybe it's a matter of chronological snobbery.

SUZANNE: What's that?

NICK: Think about it. It's the bias that whatever is newest is best. So whichever is the latest discovery must be the final word. But that's pretty obnoxious.

SUZANNE: I'm not following.

NICK: Look, for years, skeptics like your Dr. Young made fun of people who accepted the Bible as historically accurate because they believed in the Hittites.

SUZANNE: The people mentioned in the Old Testament?

NICK: Right. Up until . . . I forget how many years ago . . . there was no archeological evidence that these people ever existed. So some scholars concluded that the Bible made them up and, therefore, it couldn't be trusted. Then there was this major discovery of a whole sophisticated civilization of Hittites, complete with a really complex language system and stuff like that.

SUZANNE: Are there any other things like that?

NICK: Lots. But I don't remember them all right now. I just remember I was impressed with the number of times something like that left the skeptics with egg on their faces. Maybe we just need to suspend judgment on things that don't yet have all the archeology behind it. I think there's a tendency to assume that the people back then who wrote the Bible must not have been very smart because they existed so long ago.

SUZANNE: But don't you think we're smarter today, with all the advances in technology and science?

NICK: Smarter? I don't think so. More informed? Yes. There's a big difference.

SUZANNE: So you're saying that the Bible really is all that my pastor says it is—inspired, authoritative, God's word, and all that?

NICK: I don't know all the stuff your pastor says or believes. The Bible does claim to be inspired.

SUZANNE: Oh, that's impressive. Hello? Clue phone? Ever hear of circular reasoning?

NICK: Give me a break, Suzanne! You didn't even let me finish my thought.

SUZANNE: Sorry.

NICK: I know it could be seen as circular reasoning. Yes, I think the Bible is inspired, but not just because it claims to be inspired.

SUZANNE: You'd be amazed at how many Christians think that's all the argument they need.

NICK: Okay. You've made your point—some Christians are simpletons. It's about time you stop writing off the whole religion just because of an anti-intellectual few.

SUZANNE: Few? You're obviously new to this religion. It's the majority, Nick.

NICK: Even if you're right, that doesn't make it legit to dismiss the whole faith system. You need to respond to Dr. Young's points with the best answers, not the most brainless ones.

SUZANNE: Like whose answers?

NICK: Did Dr. Young have you read any of C. S. Lewis's stuff for his class?

SUZANNE: No, we only read Albert Schweitzer and *The Da Vinci Code.*

NICK: *The Da Vinci Code*? A work of fiction? Did you read any of the New Testament—in a class called "Intro to the New Testament"?

SUZANNE: Not very much of it. I was surprised.

NICK: And you're telling me this professor is evenhanded?

SUZANNE: Okay. Now it's time for you to get off your high horse. *The Da Vinci Code* is not all that bad. He's a great writer.

NICK: But having you read something that doesn't even *claim* to be factual stacks the deck a bit. Don't you think?

SUZANNE: I think *The Da Vinci Code* claims to be historical fiction.

NICK: Does it sound plausible to you?

SUZANNE: Not really.

NICK: Some new books have come out that show just how bogus his supposed facts are. The same thing goes with Albert Schweitzer. His stuff was shown to be full of holes a long time ago.

SUZANNE: But all your arguments assume that there's a right way to interpret things. I don't know if I buy that anymore. I think words are unreliable.

NICK: Do you expect me to believe that?

SUZANNE: Of course. Why shouldn't I?

NICK: Because you used words to tell it to me.

SUZANNE: Yeah, but words can mean anything. It's all up to the reader to decide what something means.

NICK: Listen, Suzanne, I took that intro to lit class too. The one where they tell you that texts have no meaning. But they still make you read them! Why bother, if they have no meaning?

SUZANNE: You think there's a right way to understand the Bible?

NICK: Yes. And so do you.

SUZANNE: No I don't.

NICK: Sure you do. The very fact that you're using words and expecting me to understand them shows that you think there's a right and a wrong way to interpret things.

SUZANNE: It made more sense when I was sitting in that lit class.

NICK: Did you have to write any papers in that class?

SUZANNE: Sure.

NICK: Did your teacher grade them?

SUZANNE: Of course.

NICK: And everyone got A's, right?

SUZANNE: No. Actually she was a really tough grader. I got a couple of C's from her.

NICK: How?

SUZANNE: How could I get a C?

NICK: Okay. Let's quit this line of argument. You're not seeing my point. If your professor said words have no meaning, I don't see why she made you write any of them down.

SUZANNE: Somehow I don't think I could appeal to that to improve my grade.

NICK: I don't think so, either. But if you're going to tell me that words have no meaning, don't expect me to have any idea what in the world you're talking about. Until you find some other way to communicate.

SUZANNE: Man, did we ever get off the point. Go back to what you were saying about C. S. Lewis.

NICK: Have you ever read his *Mere Christianity*?

SUZANNE: No.

NICK: You might consider it worth reading. Anyway, the fact that the Bible claims its own inspiration isn't conclusive, but it should be part of our taking the book seriously. Shoot, *The Da Vinci Code* doesn't even claim to be true and your professor assigns it as a textbook. But the Bible does make a ton of claims about itself, and Dr. Skeptic only assigns excerpts.

SUZANNE: Calm down. So what else about the Bible, besides its own self-promotion, makes you so positive it's inspired?

NICK: Positive? I never said I'm positive. I think a lot of Christians back themselves into a corner by claiming

to be positive of things. I'd use the word *confident*—
I'm confident about certain things. I don't like it
when Christians talk about "proofs"—proofs for the
existence of God, the inspiration of the Bible, and
other things. To me, it makes more sense to talk about
factors that point us toward confidence, rather than
proofs that make us sure.

SUZANNE: That's refreshing. I like that.

NICK: So I'd say there are some *factors* for believing the
Bible. I already mentioned that it just seems plausible
that God could, if he wanted to, reveal stuff to us. It
seems that looking inside ourselves for the answers
to the deepest questions of life is exactly the wrong
place to look. We need input from the outside—from
the God who made us—rather than from the inside,
where we're all kind of mixed up. That's one factor.
I can think of two others—the fact that the Bible is
such a mess and the fact that it's insulting.

SUZANNE: A mess?

NICK: Yeah. You know—all those places that bother
you the most and tend to make Christians a little
embarrassed. Those are exactly the places that make
me think it must be accurate.

SUZANNE: I'm not following you yet.

NICK: Look, if you were writing the Bible as a slick
propaganda piece, you'd leave out some stuff—like
all those things that people think are contradictions.
There *are* explanations that will smooth them out, but
I don't want to get into all that right now. The point
is, people do need to smooth them out.

SUZANNE: Give me an example, please.

NICK: Okay. One gospel says Jesus was walking into Jericho
when he did some miracle. Another gospel says
he was walking out of it. Scholars say this isn't a
contradiction because, told from a Jewish point of

view, Jericho's city limit was one place, but told from a Gentile point of view, the limit was somewhere else. Imagine that—Jews and Gentiles in Israel disagreeing about land! So what else is new? The point is, one gospel writer was talking to Jews, so he uses one boundary and says Jesus was walking In. The other is looking from a different point of view. Get it? It's confusing and I'm not even trying to convince you that's the best way to resolve the tension. What I'm trying to say is, if the Bible was some concocted piece of PR, the writers would have smoothed out this mess. The fact that the conflict is still in there means that the writers just accurately recorded what happened and let the chips fall where they may.

SUZANNE: Got a better example?

NICK: Well, the resurrection is a really big deal in the New Testament. But if you were making up that story to convince people that Jesus was the Messiah, you would've avoided the stumbling blocks. Like this one—the first people to get to the empty tomb and start claiming that Jesus rose from the dead were women! Don't take this the wrong way, Suzanne, but women weren't considered reliable witnesses back then. They weren't even allowed to testify in court as eyewitnesses. But Matthew, Mark, Luke, and John all say that women showed up first. Saying that didn't help their case—they just recorded it that way because that's the way it really happened.

SUZANNE: This is interesting. The very things that Christians are always trying to smooth over should actually be used to show the Bible's inspiration.

NICK: And there are lots of things like that in both Testaments. And the fact that the Bible is such a conglomeration of things—stories, sermons, poems, things written by so many different people at different times. It's a mess—just like people! We're a mixture of logic, emotion, memories, dreams, with different moods and conflicting ideas. The Bible is the perfect mess for us.

SUZANNE: You make me want to read it again.

NICK: Cool.

SUZANNE: Don't let it go to your head. And what did you mean that the Bible's insulting?

NICK: If you just wanted to tell a story that would sell, the Bible wouldn't be what you'd come up with.

SUZANNE: Why not?

NICK: What do you think the Bible's about? What's its big idea?

SUZANNE: I've always answered that question with something like, "love" or "God's love for us." I remember our youth group leader doing this thing about the Bible being God's love letter to us. It seemed really stupid at the time. I guess it still does.

NICK: A rather long, complex love letter, that's for sure.

SUZANNE: I guess I'm not sure how to answer your question. What do you think the Bible's main theme is?

NICK: When I first started reading that New Testament that came in the Freshman Welcome Pack, I immediately got confused. I felt like I was picking up some book in the middle of the story. So I asked my roommate what part of the drama I'd missed and why did it seem like I was being dropped into the middle of the story.

SUZANNE: Way to go, Nick. Wasn't your roommate one of the people giving these packs out?

NICK: Exactly. So I figured he'd have some reason why they were giving out just the New Testament instead of the whole Bible.

SUZANNE: What'd he say?

NICK: He was pretty cool about it. He said I was probably right and that his group should consider giving out the whole Bible. The problem is, most people won't read that much and would just get turned off and not read anything.

SUZANNE: That probably depends on which college you're at.

NICK: Could be. I suggested they give out some kind of one-page thing that gives an overview of the whole Bible, and then suggest places for people to read.

SUZANNE: And let me guess. He asked you to come up with such a thing.

NICK: Not yet.

SUZANNE: Well . . . now that you're a Bible scholar . . .

NICK: Very funny. Listen, I don't know what the one point of the Bible is. But I think it's got to include the idea of redemption. That might be the thing that holds it all together. Almost from the very beginning, there's this need for reconciliation between God and people. All the way through the Bible, you get this sense that what should have been a close relationship somehow went wrong.

SUZANNE: Like a bad marriage.

NICK: Only worse. God is the faithful, loving husband, and we're all the cheating wife.

SUZANNE: I think you're right. Even though I've never heard anyone put it that way.

NICK: So the Old Testament combines God's judgment on us and his promise to save us from our own stupidity.

SUZANNE: Isn't it really a lot worse than stupidity?

NICK: Good point. Our problem includes a lot more than stupidity. If we were just stupid or ignorant, all we'd need is information.

SUZANNE: That's kind of what Dr. Young implied. And it's the one thing I just never bought from him. It sounded like he was saying that to find real truth we just need to enlighten our minds.

NICK: He's not alone. Lots of people are saying that—and it's

	not a new message, either, although it sells like crazy. Just look at all the self-help books in a bookstore.
SUZANNE:	That was the one part of my Christian upbringing that *did* stick—and I don't think I was brainwashed into thinking I'm some kind of sinful wretch.
NICK:	Some churches do overemphasize that.
SUZANNE:	Yeah, but that doesn't mean there isn't some truth in it. If I'm really honest with myself, I have to admit there's some real ugly stuff inside my heart.
NICK:	Exactly. So what we need isn't just information. We need transformation.
SUZANNE:	Redemption's even better, I think.
NICK:	Right—'cause it's a relationship word. We don't just need to be made right inside ourselves. We also need to be made right with God.
SUZANNE:	Mmm. So the reason you say the Bible is insulting is because it doesn't say we just need enlightenment?
NICK:	Yes. Telling me I need to be enlightened makes me want to learn so I can feel even better about myself. Telling me I need to be redeemed makes me either reject your message and get even prouder about myself, or it makes me want to say, "Yeah. You're right. I do need to humble myself and get some kind of overhaul."
SUZANNE:	I also think some people reject the message of the Bible because they don't want to stop some things they're doing—things that they know are wrong. It's like, "If I believe this redemption message, I'll probably have to stop sleeping around or getting drunk or whatever."
NICK:	I think you're right, but that's getting away from the point I was trying to make.
SUZANNE:	Sorry. I was just replaying some of the most disturbing moments in my New Testament class. It was almost like Dr. Young was giving people

permission to sin when he punched holes in the Bible. Like, if the Bible really isn't what it claims to be, then there's no right and wrong and we can just do whatever we want.

NICK: And some atheists will actually admit that. Aldous Huxley once said that he wanted the world to have no meaning so it would be okay for him to be sexually and politically liberated.

SUZANNE: Wow. I assume you could show me where he said that, if I wanted you to.

NICK: Yeah. The point is—the Bible's insulting because it tells us stuff we'd rather not hear. But that's also what makes it so good.

SUZANNE: Kind of like bad tasting medicine—it's what you need to get healthy instead of sweet tasting candy that only makes you feel better about being sick.

NICK: Only more so. But you're seeing my point.

SUZANNE: I think you *should* be the one to write that intro-to-the-Bible piece for those Freshman Welcome Packs.

NICK: I don't know about that. I'm just struggling to figure this stuff out.

SUZANNE: That's exactly why I think you should do it. You're closer to the problem than a lot of Christians—the ones who've been Christian for so long they don't remember why they believe the Bible. What would you put on that one-page summary?

NICK: My idea actually isn't as original as you think. I like what Dr. Hart once said in one of his lectures about the Bible. The whole story line of the Bible could be summed up by remembering C-R-R-C.

SUZANNE: Go on.

NICK: Creation-Rebellion-Redemption-Consummation.

SUZANNE: Rebellion sounds kind of harsh.

NICK: It is—but I think it *has* to be that harsh. God created the world, with us as the high point of his creation, and then we tell him to go take a hike—that we don't need him anymore, or that we'd rather build our world around ourselves instead of seeing that he's built the whole world around himself.

SUZANNE: I still don't like the word *rebellion*.

NICK: I don't *like* it either—but it's a true picture of our sin. The good news is that the story doesn't stop there. Creation, then rebellion, but then comes redemption. God sent Jesus to pay for our sins and buy us back for God.

SUZANNE: And that's why they give out the New Testament in those packs.

NICK: I guess.

SUZANNE: And consummation?

NICK: That's where it all comes together in the end. The story begins with God creating the heavens and the earth, and in the end he creates the new heavens and the new earth.

SUZANNE: You sound so sure of yourself, Nick. I mean, you sound so sure of the Bible. Don't you have any doubts about it?

NICK: Tons. I'm really sorry if I sound like a know-it-all. I hate it when people sound like they've got more answers than God does. I've got a lot of doubts about the Bible. It's just that the good stuff I've found out about it outweighs any of my doubts.

SUZANNE: Like what kind of doubts do you have?

NICK: Mostly just stuff I don't understand. Like the entire book of Hebrews. I can't figure out how all those sacrifices fit in. And I tried reading Revelations—

SUZANNE: It's just Revelation, not Revelations.

NICK: Sorry. Whatever it's called, I can't figure out a word of it. This girl down the hall gave me a bunch of *Left Behind* books. She said they'd help me understand Revelation. But they didn't.

SUZANNE: So there's a bunch of stuff about the Bible you don't
            understand. Join the club. That's not what I'm talking
            about. I mean real problems with the Bible. Stuff you
            do understand but don't like.

NICK: Oh . . . like when that guy got killed by God simply
            because he didn't rest on the Sabbath?

SUZANNE: Exactly.

NICK: Or why some cities got destroyed by Israel in such
            disgusting ways.

SUZANNE: Yeah. Things like that.

NICK: I don't have any answers for you. I found those things
            really disturbing. I've read some stuff on the Internet
            that tries to explain why God works that way—
            because he's so holy or something—but it didn't
            satisfy me. Yeah, I still have a lot of questions. And
            they're not just intellectual ones. I'm really bothered
            by a lot things.

SUZANNE: But . . . ?

NICK: But what?

SUZANNE: I thought you might be about to say, "I'm really bothered
            but I'm still going to become a Christian and not worry
            about those things." Is that what you're saying?

NICK: Maybe. I'd say I'm really close. My roommate is really
            cool about not pushing me. He did say that he wants
            to be at my baptism, whenever I do make the move.
            But he's never put any pressure on.

SUZANNE: You're lucky.

NICK: I guess what I'm saying is that most of the Bible
            impresses me as something pretty easy to understand
            and really good. The hard stuff is the exception rather
            than the rule. I guess some day I might find answers
            to more of my questions.

SUZANNE: It almost seems like God goes through this major
            makeover and becomes nice in the New Testament
            after being so nasty in the Old.

NICK: Almost. I thought that for a while, and one of the
           guys in our Bible study is always saying that. But I
           don't know. That just doesn't sound right.

SUZANNE: Why not?

NICK: At first glance, it looks like God is mean in the Old
           Testament and nice in the New. But the more I read,
           the more it seems like God is both righteous and
           gracious all the way through, and he seems to get
           more of each as the Bible progresses.

SUZANNE: So you're saying God is maturing?

NICK: No. I know it *sounds* like I just said that. But I don't
           think God changes any. I think we just get to see more
           about him as time goes on.

SUZANNE: How can you say God is gracious in the Old
           Testament?

NICK: Are you kidding? Look at how patient he is with
           the people of Israel all the way through the Old
           Testament—even though they keep screwing up. He
           didn't zap all of 'em there in the desert after getting
           them out of Egypt—that shows a lot of patience. Or
           when they complained that, "At least we used to have
           garlic to eat back in Egypt." God seems more patient
           than I can imagine. And then he goes and sends them
           food from heaven, and protects them against enemies.
           Sometimes I wonder if God is even more gracious in
           the Old Testament than in the New Testament.

SUZANNE: Yeah, but isn't God so much less nasty in the New
           Testament?

NICK: I don't think so. Go ask those two people who died in
           the book of Acts because they didn't give their money
           to God. What were their names again?

SUZANNE: Is that Ananias and Sapphira?

NICK: Yeah. That's them.

SUZANNE: But they're only two. That doesn't compare to all the
           people God kills in the Old Testament.

NICK: I guess. But it's not just body count. It's the intensity
            of the language. I think the harshest and most
            descriptive words about hell and punishment all come
            in the New Testament—and most of them come from
            the mouth of Jesus. It seems to me, too, that all the
            themes of God's character traits increase and come to
            a high point in Revelation. That's the one part of *that*
            book I did understand. God's descriptions of both his
            love and his punishments are the clearest at the end of
            the Bible.

SUZANNE: How often did you go to that Christian Studies
            Center? It sounds like they brainwashed you really
            well.

NICK: Brainwashed?

SUZANNE: That was mean. Sorry.

NICK: I did spend a lot of time there.

SUZANNE: It sounds like you like what you're learning.

NICK: Yeah.

SUZANNE: I guess we both still have some doubts.

NICK: Lots.

SUZANNE: What was the name of that book you kept mentioning
            a while ago? *Mirror Christianity*?

NICK: *Mere Christianity* by C. S. Lewis.

SUZANNE: That's it. I'll tell you what. Let's make a deal. I'll read
            that book this summer and you read *The Da Vinci
            Code* and we'll talk about them.

NICK: I think that'd be great.

SUZANNE: Only . . . we talk about them somewhere else. You
            may like wings a lot but look at our plates. You've got
            a mountain of bones from your wings and I've got,
            like, three wings worth.

NICK: We can order more. They're only a quarter!

SUZANNE: It's not the money—it's the grease. If we're going to
            talk about this any more, it's got to be some place
            where I can get a salad.

NICK:　　　　They've got salads here!

SUZANNE:　　They've also got smoke. How do you stand it in here?
　　　　　　　I feel like I just smoked a pack and half of cigarettes.

NICK:　　　　I'd put up with a lot for twenty-five-cent wings.

SUZANNE:　　Uh-uh. Next time, I pick the place.

NICK:　　　　Deal.

❖

Keep the Conversation Going

- The biblical passage that would be most helpful is . . . well . . .
  the whole Bible. If that seems a bit much, try the first book—
  Genesis. It will introduce you to God, the way he works, and
  his way of revealing himself to people.
- A helpful Web site addressing the topic of this chapter, and
  those raised elsewhere in this book, is Stand to Reason at
  www.str.org.
- Another online resource for these sorts of questions is www
  .leaderu.com.
- A good source of defense about the New Testament's reliability
  can be found in J. P. Moreland, *Scaling the Secular City: A
  Defense of Christianity* (Grand Rapids: Baker, 1987), 133–58.

  50　*Exactly. And there are these charts*: See Josh McDowell,
  　　*The New Evidence That Demands a Verdict: Fully
  　　Updated in One Volume to Answer Questions
  　　Challenging Christians in the 21st Century* (Nashville:
  　　Nelson, 1999), 38.

  53　*The Bible does claim to be inspired*: See 2 Timothy
  　　3:16–17.

  54　*Some new books have come out that show just how
  　　bogus his supposed facts are*: For example, Darrell Bock,
  　　*Breaking the Da Vinci Code: Answers to the Questions
  　　Everyone's Asking* (Nashville: Nelson, 2004).

Also, www.leaderu.com has some helpful articles about Albert Schweitzer.

55   *Have you ever read his* Mere Christianity?: C. S. Lewis, *Mere Christianity* (reprint, San Francisco: Harper, 2001).

61   *And some atheists will actually admit that*: Aldous Huxley, *Ends and Means: An Inquiry into the Nature of Ideals and into the Methods Employed for Their Realization* (Westport: Greenwood, 1969), 270.

63   *Like when that guy got killed by God simply because he didn't rest on the Sabbath?*: See Numbers 15:32–36. Just one of many commentaries that address this passage is Gordon J. Wenham, *Numbers: An Introduction and Commentary* (Downers Grove, Ill.: InterVarsity, 1981), 131. Some helpful answers to similar difficult questions can be found in Peter H. Davids et al., *Hard Sayings of the Bible* (Downers Grove, Ill.: InterVarsity, 1996).

Across from Grace Community Church

A Two-Way Discussion About One Way to Heaven

WHEN THIRTY ADULTS AND TWELVE CHILDREN first started meeting in the Boynton Elementary School cafeteria, no one noticed or cared. But Grace Community Church, as they called themselves, grew to over two hundred people in less than a year. Then parking in the school lot began to overflow into the surrounding neighborhood. When the congestion started slowing residents down on their way to the golf course or brunch buffets, they took notice.

Now, five years later, GCC's new building takes up residence on the corner of Elm and Macketeer streets. Everyone in town knows someone who attends the contemporary, upbeat, "Grace Place." But no one knows how to peg this church. It has no denominational ties, no stained glass windows, no sign outside with the week's sermon title, and no advertisements for bingo. People on both sides of the political spectrum say they feel at home there. GCC sets up a booth at every community fair or gathering, where they offer the most fun games for kids, the most intriguing literature for adults, and the most helpful relief for families with special needs or financial difficulties.

Kids love it at GCC. Their youth center, complete with a full-court gym, coffee bar, and rockin' music is a big draw for Turnerville's high school crowd.

Bob Mellon started attending GCC the first Easter they were in their new building. A coworker invited him and his wife, Julie, and they had no good reason to decline the invitation. They could have just slept in that Sunday—the way they had every other Sunday throughout their four years of marriage and two prior years of living together. Religion was simply irrelevant for them. But after that Easter service, they liked the church experience and felt like the pastor crafted his sermon exactly for them. They haven't missed a Sunday since.

Bob's neighborhood friend Gregg did find a way to decline Bob's Easter service invitation this year. The two had known each other for years and now met regularly to play basketball at the community center gym. Gregg was one of the groomsmen in Bob and Julie's wedding and had noticed the change in their Sunday morning routine. Gregg even sensed some changes in Bob's whole outlook on life. It wasn't a stretch for Gregg to link GCC and Bob's new attitude. But Gregg used the word irrelevant to describe religion, just as Bob had done for years. So he politely told Bob that he already had family plans for Easter and said in a slightly patronizing way, "Maybe next year."

As the two met for coffee before work at the Starbucks across the street from Grace Community's new building, the conversation quite naturally turned to spiritual matters.

❖

BOB:	Hey, are we on for hoops tomorrow night?
GREGG:	I think so. Let me check my work schedule when I get to the office. I might have to work late, and that would throw things off a bit. But I'm pretty sure it can work.
BOB:	Great. I missed last week and I can tell. I need the exercise.
GREGG:	That's right. You missed last time. Where were you again? Some church thing?
BOB:	It was a seminar our church did about communication in marriage. It was really good.
GREGG:	You and Julie doing okay?

BOB: Never better—really. But we can always use help with
            communication, like any couple. The people who did
            this seminar were really funny . . . hysterical.

GREGG: That church has been a big deal for you guys,
            hasn't it?

BOB: Yeah. I'd say it's changed our life more than anything
            else.

GREGG: That's great. Really. I just wish other Christians I
            know weren't so judgmental. I mean . . . you're not.
            But you're not the norm. Why is that? Why aren't you
            like them?

BOB: I can't speak for them. Maybe they judge you because
            you put so much sugar in your coffee. How can you
            drink stuff like that?

GREGG: Very funny. I'm serious about this. Look out the
            window at that red Buick. You see its bumper sticker?

BOB: Yeah, I see it. Nice and subtle. "Next time you think
            you're perfect, try walking on water."

GREGG: I hate that. I don't think I'm perfect. I just don't
            buy all the religious stuff a lot of born-againers do.
            That's the right term, isn't it—*born-again*? You'd call
            yourself a born-again Christian, wouldn't you?

BOB: For the past two years, yes.

GREGG: But I never get any of that holier-than-thou feeling
            from you, like I do from people with those bumper
            stickers, or those fish symbols on the back of their
            cars—the ones with the Christian fish eating the
            Darwin one.

BOB: Or how about my favorite bumper sticker: "If you're
            living like there is no God, you'd better be right."

GREGG: Exactly. I mean, I think it's all right to believe
            anything, as long as it works for you.

BOB: Really? Anything?

GREGG: Okay. Those wackos who killed themselves a couple
            of years ago when that comet flew by—they're the

exception. But all the major religions are all basically good.

BOB: Wackos? Basically good? Now who's being judgmental?

GREGG: What do you mean?

BOB: When you say that those wackos were wrong—and I agree with you—you're making an evaluation. Maybe born-again Christians do the same thing. It's just that you don't like their evaluation.

GREGG: I'm not telling anyone they're going to hell! It sounds like Christians think everyone who disagrees with them is going to hell. Do you believe that?

BOB: Do you believe in hell?

GREGG: Hmm. I don't know. I doubt it.

BOB: Then why is this such a big deal to you?

GREGG: I don't follow.

BOB: Why do you care about who I think is or isn't going to hell—if there really isn't such a place?

GREGG: Well . . . suppose I did believe in hell. Actually, I think I do. I mean, I don't think Hitler's in heaven.

BOB: Good point.

GREGG: So let's say there is a hell. Do you think anyone who's not a Christian is going to hell?

BOB: Let's back up a minute. Christianity isn't the only religion that thinks it's the only right way to God, you know. Pretty much every religion claims to be right. Why else would anyone believe it? Who's going to follow a religion that makes no claims to being right?

GREGG: Okay.

BOB: So if some religions say their way is right, they exclude people who believe some other way.

GREGG: I don't follow.

BOB: I'll give you an example—and there are a lot of them. Christianity and Judaism—and Islam, for that matter—all believe there's only one God. And it's a pretty big deal to them that people worship him. And it's an even bigger deal that people don't worship any other god, or thing, or person, or whatever else you might want to fix your affections on.

GREGG: Like my dad and his ridiculous obsession with cars. He's a fanatic.

BOB: There you go sounding judgmental again. Are you sure you're not a born-again something or other?

GREGG: Go on.

BOB: Judaism thinks one of the worst things you can do is worship something that doesn't deserve worship. It's an affront to God. It would be like you telling your wife that she's the most important woman in the world to you, but you take some other babe out to dinner that night. Do you see my point?

GREGG: Sounds like God is jealous.

BOB: Not a bad word choice! Do you think that's a problem?

GREGG: Yeah, I do. I think jealousy is a kind of weakness.

BOB: Would your wife be "weak" if she were jealous because you took some other woman out to dinner? Or would she just be doing what's right in light of how important your marriage is? Doesn't jealousy make sense when you're guarding something precious?

GREGG: I'm beginning to get your point.

BOB: You'd really get my point if I told the story the other way around—like if she were going out to dinner with some other guy. Would your jealousy be a sign of weakness?

GREGG: Got it.

BOB: Then how much more valid is jealousy when we're talking about the God of the universe? He wants people to do what only makes sense—worship him.

GREGG: How'd we get down this rabbit trail? I think I lost you.

BOB: Sorry. I did wander a bit. I was trying to say that *all* religions are kind of narrow—not just Christianity. Some religions say there's only one god. Some say there are tons . . . like Hinduism. Some religions, like Judaism, say God is personal. Some say God is just an impersonal force . . . like in Buddhism. They can't all be right.

GREGG: Aren't those differences kind of minor?

BOB: Are you kidding? One versus many? Personal versus impersonal?

GREGG: But why can't they all get along? That's *my* bumper sticker! Why can't they just say you've got your way to god and I've got my way?

BOB: How narrow-minded of you!

GREGG: What? That's not narrow-minded! That's open-minded.

BOB: Except to everyone who disagrees with that plan.

GREGG: How so?

BOB: Your "every way is okay" religion is amazingly intolerant of every religion that thinks it's the only way. You just told every Christian in the world that their religion is wrong—you narrow-minded fanatic.

GREGG: I've got a headache. I'm going to get some more coffee. Want anything?

BOB: No thanks. Don't forget the sugar!

GREGG: Ha. Ha.

❖

The conversation resumes after Gregg returns with his refill.

❖

BOB: Look. I realize this is a little confusing. I'm okay about changing the subject, if you'd rather.

GREGG: No. This is fine. But I do need to leave in about fifteen minutes.

BOB:	Me too.
GREGG:	Go back to what you were just saying—about how I'm the intolerant one.
BOB:	Maybe we should define *tolerance*. We might be using the same word to mean different things.
GREGG:	Tolerance means that you accept everyone without judging.
BOB:	Wow. I think you just made things worse. *Accept. Judge.* Those are loaded words.
GREGG:	I don't think so. You're making this too complicated. I just mean I shouldn't tell anyone they're wrong for believing what they believe.
BOB:	Now we're back where we started. Didn't you say those people who killed themselves when the comet flew by were wrong?
GREGG:	Yeah.
BOB:	Then you're not very tolerant.
GREGG:	Okay. I'm stuck. How would you define tolerance?
BOB:	I wouldn't even use that word. It's gotten too messed up by people using it the wrong way. I guess, technically, if you tolerate something, you still disagree with it to some extent. Like your body—it builds a tolerance to some harmful substances that don't agree with it. If you agree with something or you're neutral about it, there's no tolerance involved.
GREGG:	Sounds like you're saying that when people use the word *tolerance*, what they really mean is *agreement* or *endorsement*.
BOB:	That might be a bit strong, but yes, what they mean is a lot more than merely tolerating something.
GREGG:	I think you're right. I'll try a different word than tolerance. What do you suggest?
BOB:	I'm not sure I can do it with just one word—how about . . . disagreeing respectfully?
GREGG:	*Disagreeing* sounds judgmental to me.

BOB: That's another word that needs definition—
          judging—but I'll save that for another cup of coffee.
GREGG: Good.
BOB: I just think that people of different religions can
          disagree and, in fact, they have to. But they should
          express their differences respectfully.
GREGG: Fine. But I'm still stuck on this exclusive thing.
          I've always thought that blind-men-and-the-
          elephant story was a pretty good explanation for the
          differences in religion.
BOB: You mean the one about the six blind guys who all
          find an elephant? They think they know what a whole
          elephant looks like.
GREGG: Right. One guy's got only the tail so he thinks an
          elephant is like a snake. And another guy's got only the
          tusk so he thinks an elephant is like a spear. Isn't that
          what different religions are like—parts of the whole?
BOB: Could be—but how would you know?
GREGG: Hmm?
BOB: The only way you'd know that one guy got just *part* of
          the elephant is if you assumed that a *whole* elephant
          did exist.
GREGG: Yeah. So?
BOB: So how can you say that there *is* a whole elephant?
          Aren't you supposed to be just one of the blind men?
          Or did whoever told this story the first time claim
          some level of knowledge for himself that he's not
          willing to give to those blind men?
GREGG: I never thought of that.
BOB: And isn't there something just a little condescending
          about saying that all these religions are blind but the
          guy telling the story can see? So who's the judgmental
          one in that story?
GREGG: I get it. I just have a hard time believing Christianity's
          the only way to God.

BOB: Maybe we should try to look at it from another angle.
            Why do you think Jesus claimed to be the only way?

GREGG: Did he really do that? Or is that just the way people
            interpreted him?

BOB: There are lots of examples of him claiming to be the
            only way. And I don't see any other way to interpret it.
            He said, "I am the way and the truth and the life. No
            one comes to the Father except through me."

GREGG: That does sound like it, I guess.

BOB: He said all sorts of outrageous things about himself,
            Gregg. Did you ever read that part of the New
            Testament I gave you?

GREGG: I started to but I . . . kind of ran out of gas.

BOB: I understand, but it wouldn't hurt to restart. You'd
            read things there that would shake up the view that
            Jesus is just a good teacher. One time he claimed to
            have the power to forgive sins, and people understood
            exactly what he was saying—that he had the same
            power as God. So they tried to stone him. And I
            could go on and on. He was always getting himself in
            trouble, saying things that made people want to kill
            him. That's not a misunderstanding on their part.
            They knew he was claiming to be God and the only
            way to God.

GREGG: I remember you telling me all this before. Jesus was
            either a liar or a lunatic or he was who he said he
            was. That makes sense to me. It still bothers me,
            though.

BOB: It bothers me too.

GREGG: What? You love this one-way stuff. Why does it bother
            you?

BOB: Here's what I mean. If Jesus is the only way, it's
            because he's the only one who died to pay for sins.
            All the other religious leaders gave people rules to
            live by, or instructions to make themselves better or

things like that. The basic idea is that if people do these things, they'll arrive at some level of whatever— holiness, heaven, Nirvana, enlightenment—some kind of goal.

GREGG: Okay.

BOB: But if Jesus is right—then it means that all those self-improvement religions don't work. It's like he's saying our problem is too deep for any of those other solutions to work. The only way we can be made right is for him to die for us. That's pretty humbling.

GREGG: How so?

BOB: Say you go to a doctor with a spot on your arm. You hope he can give you some kind of ointment to rub on the spot to make it go away, or maybe some pill you can take that kills the infection. But you go there and he does some tests, and then he says there's some big cancerous infection under the skin. The only way to stop it from killing you is by cutting off the arm. You're going to feel pretty overwhelmed.

GREGG: Or get a second opinion.

BOB: Sure. But suppose the second opinion . . . and third and fourth and fiftieth all tell you the same thing. It means your problem is a whole lot worse than you thought.

GREGG: So you're saying that our sin is like cancer?

BOB: And worse! And other religions don't think it's that bad. That's why I kind of wish they were right. But Christianity is the only one that really squares with reality, I think. The problem of my sin really is that bad.

GREGG: Really? You really think you're that bad?

BOB: Only because of how good God is. If I'm just comparing myself to other people, I'm pretty good, especially if I compare myself to someone like you— you sinful wretch.

GREGG: Hey!

BOB: Okay. You're not a wretch.

GREGG: I think some of this is making sense.

BOB: Parts of Christianity are pretty different than the way
            I'd always thought. But I do think it makes more sense.

GREGG: But aren't some people really good? I mean, like
            Gandhi or someone like that.

BOB: People always talk about Gandhi being so good. Why
            is that?

GREGG: He was good, wasn't he? I mean, all that non-violence
            stuff.

BOB: Well sure. He was a great man. He just wasn't as good
            or as holy as most people want to believe. Even *he*
            didn't think he was good enough to go to heaven.

GREGG: Really?

BOB: Did you ever read his autobiography? He said
            something like, "It is an unbroken torture to me that I
            am still so far from him, who as I fully know, governs
            every breath of my life, and whose offspring I am."

GREGG: Wow. I never heard that.

BOB: I'm not on some anti-Gandhi thing. He did a lot of
            good. But when it comes to the game of "goodness,"
            we just have to see the playing field differently. We're
            not comparing ourselves to just a bunch of people.
            We're comparing ourselves to the standard of God's
            goodness and rightness. When we do that, it's a whole
            different game.

GREGG: That *is* different.

BOB: You know what I think? I think Christianity is a voice
            of humility in an age of arrogance.

GREGG: Now I think you need more coffee. How can you say
            Christianity is humble if it claims to be the only way
            to God?

BOB: Let me ask you a question. Do you think you're going
            to heaven?

GREGG:	I guess.
BOB:	Do you think everybody goes to heaven?
GREGG:	I don't think so.
BOB:	You already said you don't think Hitler's in heaven, right?
GREGG:	Right. And there are others like him who won't be in heaven.
BOB:	Why do you think you're going to heaven?
GREGG:	Hmm . . . 'cause I'm a pretty good person. I never killed anyone. I don't cheat on my wife. You know.
BOB:	So you'll get to heaven because you've been a pretty good person but some people will go to hell because they've been pretty bad.
GREGG:	Yeah . . . I think. I'm not sure.
BOB:	So you think you're better than the people who go to hell?
GREGG:	I guess.
BOB:	You see? That's why I say that Christianity is a voice of humility in an age of arrogance. Your view sounds more arrogant. You think you're better than other people. But Christianity says that no one's good enough to get to heaven.
GREGG:	No one?
BOB:	No one.
GREGG:	Not even Mother Teresa?
BOB:	Nope.
GREGG:	You're telling me that Mother Teresa's not in heaven?
BOB:	I didn't say that.
GREGG:	Yes, you did. You just said that no one's good enough to get to heaven.
BOB:	Right. So if Mother Teresa's in heaven it's not because she's good enough. It's because God is gracious to her. It's because she's counting on Christ's Cross and not on her acts of kindness to dying people in Calcutta.
GREGG:	I need some time to digest this.

BOB: I know. This is counterintuitive. I had to wrestle with
                it for a long time before it sunk in. Here's another way
                to think about it: The only way people get to heaven is
                by accepting a gift—not be being good enough. That's
                humble. Thinking you're good enough is arrogant.

GREGG: Are you really saying that all those other religions of
                the world are out to lunch?

BOB: Not at all. I think they get a lot of it right.

GREGG: Just not all of it.

BOB: Exactly. In fact, I'd be surprised if they were totally
                crazy. I think *all* the religions of the world point in
                the same direction, and they have a lot of the same
                info on their signposts along the way.

GREGG: Like what info?

BOB: Like there really is something more to life than just
                what we see here and now. And that there's some
                kind of god that we're longing for. And that there's
                something inside of us that's incomplete without that
                god. But there's also something inside of us that's
                exactly the problem.

GREGG: You mean, what you keep calling "sin"?

BOB: It's not just me but, yes, what the Bible calls "sin."

GREGG: And different religions have different ways to solve
                the sin problem.

BOB: Right. Although, they all seem to fall into the same
                camp—people doing something to make themselves
                better or more acceptable to God—praying a certain
                prayer or doing some good deed for others or some
                kind of ritual, like bathing in the Ganges river.

GREGG: All of them?

BOB: All the ones that I'm aware of—except Christianity.
                That's the one religion that says you can bathe all day
                long in whatever river you want to—or do certain
                deeds, or pray certain prayers—and you still haven't
                gotten rid of your sin. Sin, you see, is the thing that

causes the unrest in your soul and the problems in your marriage and the desire to get drunk—and whatever else is causing you to ask questions about what life is all about.

GREGG: Couldn't there be some other system? Like getting your good deeds to outweigh your bad ones?

BOB: It's interesting that you'd want to find some other system. Why do you resist the Christian one?

GREGG: I don't know. Let me think about that.

BOB: Sure. But think about this, too—a system where the good deeds outweigh the bad? How would you measure those deeds? Do *some* really good things outweigh some okay things? And are you saying that someone who did something really bad . . . like kill someone . . . would then have to do some really great thing—like discover the cure for cancer—in order for their bad deeds to be outweighed? The whole system seems absurd after a while.

GREGG: I see what you mean. You do sound pretty sure of this stuff. How can you be so sure?

BOB: I'm not without my doubts, believe me. But I do think my whole outlook on religions has changed because of two things—one kind of logical, the other more practical.

GREGG: Go ahead.

BOB: The logical one is about Jesus' resurrection. When Julie and I first went to church together—that Easter a couple of years ago—I heard arguments about the resurrection that really convinced me that it's true. It's like a fact of history—just as factual as Washington crossing the Delaware. I could get you some stuff to read about it but here's the point—the fact that Jesus rose from the dead puts him in a whole different category than all the other religious leaders or gurus of the world. His rising from the dead

means that, if you believe in him, you'll overcome
death too.

GREGG: You think you're going to rise from the dead?

BOB: In a sense, yes. I've got confidence that I'll go to heaven
when I die. Not because I'm good enough to get there
but because I'm trusting in Christ, not myself.

GREGG: I think I'd like to read some of that stuff about the
resurrection. Is there some Web site I could look it
up on?

BOB: Definitely. Just do a Google search on "proof of the
resurrection" or something like that, and you'll find
plenty of stuff—especially any of the writings by Josh
McDowell.

GREGG: I'll check it out. You said there was something else
that changed your outlook on religion. Something
practical?

BOB: How all this changed my marriage. All this stuff about
forgiveness and sin and the resurrection—it's all kind
of theoretical. But when Julie and I started learning
this stuff—no . . . it's not just learning. That sounds too
brainy. It was like we were encountering something—
or maybe it was Someone. I don't know if I can explain
it that well. But all this stuff about experiencing
forgiveness from God started spilling over into our
forgiving each other. We started getting along better.

GREGG: I never knew you guys were having trouble.

BOB: It wasn't like major trouble. I mean we weren't
thinking of splitting up or anything. But, you know,
marriage is tough. Sometimes you just want to wring
each other's necks. And sometimes you deserve to get
shot by your spouse.

GREGG: Can you give me an example of how this works?

BOB: Fair enough. Just last night Julie and I had to talk
about something in the checkbook. She'd made a
math error and it messed things up. When I went

to go write a check, I realized there was something wrong and immediately felt like yelling at her. This kind of thing has happened before—actually, quite a few times. Every other time I've blasted her and made her feel really bad.

GREGG: You creep!

BOB. Hey. I didn't say I'm proud of it. But I do have this harsh side to me that comes out between us sometimes. For a long time I tried to solve it myself. I even went to that anger management seminar about three or four years ago. Remember that?

GREGG: Yeah. I remember thinking you were throwing your money down the drain.

BOB: Thanks. You might have been right, though. Just trying to change my behavior on the outside didn't work. That's for sure.

GREGG: So how does religion help there?

BOB: I'm not entirely sure I can put it into words. There's some kind of link, though. God forgives me, and is gentle with me when I do things far worse than making a math error in a checkbook. Then it seems like I extend—*extend* is a good word for it, I think— that same kind of grace or gentleness or whatever toward Julie . . . and that never happened before.

GREGG: Lots of people can get this same kind of training or advice *without* religion. I still don't see the connection.

BOB: We tried lots of other things. All I can tell you is that last night with both of us looking at that checkbook, there was a kind of grace working in our conflict that sure worked better than all the yelling matches we had before.

GREGG: I think I get what you're saying. I need to think about it some more. You've made some good points.

BOB: Well, you raised some good questions.

GREGG: Good. Whoa! Look at the time. Guess I better get to work, or come Friday my wife and I might be arguing over *our* checkbook balance.

BOB: Another good point.

GREGG: See ya on the basketball court tonight. I'll call you if I'm going to be late.

BOB: Great.

One week later, Bob and Gregg meet again—same place, same time, continuation of the same conversation.

BOB: You're walking pretty well for someone who got beat so bad at basketball the other night.

GREGG: Better than you'll be walking tomorrow—after tonight's game.

BOB: Talk is cheap, buddy. We'll see how things go tonight and who's walking at all tomorrow. Here, I brought you some more sugar. Hey . . . anymore thoughts about our whole religious discussion last week?

GREGG: Actually, I've been thinking about it a lot. I do have another question, though. What about people who've never heard all this stuff about Christianity? It sounds like you're saying that anyone who hasn't heard about Jesus is going to hell. That doesn't sound fair.

BOB: You're right. It doesn't. But maybe there's another way to look at it.

GREGG: How?

BOB: Your question presupposes two things. One, there actually is a message to hear, and two, some haven't heard it.

GREGG: Right.

BOB:	The Bible would say *yes* to the first presupposition—there is a message to be heard. But the Bible would say *no* to the second presupposition—there really aren't any people who haven't heard it.
GREGG:	You've got to be kidding me. There are millions of people who haven't heard about Jesus.
BOB:	Let's take one thing at a time. The Bible says there certainly is a message everyone must hear. I'll summarize it in four points. First, there is a loving, righteous, knowable God. Second, there's something about us that separates us from that God. Third, God has provided a means to reconcile us—Jesus' death on the cross. Fourth, each person needs to trust in that means of reconciliation for themselves.
GREGG:	I agree that summarizes the Christian message. I don't know if I buy it, but I think it's accurate. But how can you say that everyone's heard that?
BOB:	Don't get ahead of me. Make sure you see what's behind this message. The means that God has provided to reconcile people to himself is one where God does the providing. It's not people earning their way to God based on what they do. This is what distinguishes Christianity from all other religions.
GREGG:	I see that.
BOB:	The Bible says that every single person on the planet already knows the first two points. They see evidence of God in nature, or in their own hearts.
GREGG:	Okay. But what about points three and four?
BOB:	Let's see, this requires a little bit of putting things together. But I think the Bible says that everyone either rejects or accepts points one and two. People look at the stars or into their hearts, and they wonder if there's some kind of creator behind it all, or they don't. They also look in their own hearts and either say, "I'm in trouble" or "I'm okay."

GREGG: Where are you getting this from?

BOB: I think the best place to study this is the first
          two chapters of the book of Romans in the New
          Testament. Maybe you should read it for yourself
          before we continue this conversation.

GREGG: I'll read it, but I'd like you to go on.

BOB: Okay. I think those two chapters argue that lots of
          people reject even this little amount of revelation—
          that there is a God and we fall far short of his
          perfection.

GREGG: What do you mean, they "reject it"?

BOB: They suppress it—they choose to ignore the evidence.
          And if that's true, then it's not God who rejects them
          but they who reject God. The Bible says they are
          without excuse.

GREGG: Why would they suppress it, though?

BOB: For the same reason anyone rejects God. He's holy
          and we're not. We'd rather not deal with a God who
          makes demands on us. That's why people who *do* buy
          the idea of a god would rather worship other gods—
          the ones that aren't so holy, or so demanding, or the
          ones that say we're not accountable.

GREGG: Okay, so stop your preaching already. Suppose they
          don't suppress it?

BOB: Interesting question. I tend to think that everyone
          suppresses the truth, at least for a while. But,
          somehow, some people start responding to what God
          reveals. I don't think God explicitly tells us how he's
          going to handle every situation because that's his job,
          and he doesn't feel the need to consult with us on
          everything.

GREGG: That's a good way of putting it.

BOB: It makes sense to me if I think of it like this:
          Revelation rejected brings darkness; revelation
          received brings light.

GREGG: You've lost me there.

BOB: If people reject the first two points of revelation,
            God is simply giving them what they ask for—a
            life separated from him—darkness. They'll stay in
            darkness unless something radical happens. But for
            the people who say, "Yes, there must be something
            bigger than me and I don't match up," I think God
            will get them the rest of the story.

GREGG: So if they say yes to points one and two, he'll send
            them three and four?

BOB: Yes.

GREGG: Where does the Bible say that?

BOB: Well, lots of places say things like, "You will seek me
            and find me when you seek me with all your heart."

GREGG: So how does God get points three and four to them?

BOB: Most of the time it's through other people, but God
            is capable of bringing the rest of the story any way he
            wants to—through visions or dreams.

GREGG: Or other religions?

BOB: I don't think so. If those other religions proclaimed
            these four points, then they wouldn't be other
            religions—they'd be Christianity! If they proclaimed
            something else, they'd be saying the way to God is
            through some form of self-effort. That's exactly the
            opposite of Christianity.

GREGG: Buddhism is self-effort?

BOB: Yes. You achieve Nirvana by meditation or some
            other discipline. Every religion says some form of "Do
            this and you'll get there." They might describe *there*
            differently and they have different lists of what to do,
            but it's mostly self-effort.

GREGG: Oh yeah. You already gave me the works-versus-grace
            sermon.

BOB: The bottom line is that I don't really know how God
            will get points three and four to someone, but his

usual plan is for people to tell people. That's why there's so much in the Bible about people going all over the world to announce this message. That's why I'm telling you all this.

GREGG: I think I'll have to read that book of Romans.

BOB: Great. What time are we meeting for hoops tonight?

GREGG: Eight-thirty. You might want to bring some crutches for afterward.

BOB: Ha! We'll see about that!

❖

Keep the Conversation Going

- The biblical material most helpful with this difficult issue is the New Testament book of Romans. Ideally, this book should be read two ways: first quickly—to get the overall argument of the book—then more slowly to dig into the details of that argument.

76   *He said, "I am the way and the truth and the life. No one comes to the Father except through me"*: The reference is John 14:6. Other exclusive claims by Jesus are implied in Matthew 18:20; 28:20; Mark 2:1–12; John 3:18; 8:24, 58. Other writers of the New Testament also claimed exclusivity for Christianity—see Acts 4:12 and Colossians 1:15–20.

78   *It is an unbroken torture to me*: Mohandas K. Gandhi, *Autobiography: The Story of My Experiments with Truth* (New York: Dover, 1983), xxix.

      Christianity is a voice of humility in an age of arrogance: I am indebted to Tim Downs for this line of reasoning. Tim is the author of *Finding Common Ground* (Chicago: Moody, 1999).

81   *The logical one is about Jesus' resurrection*: Just one

of many sources of evidence for the resurrection can be found in William Lane Craig's *Reasonable Faith* (Wheaton: Crossway, 1994) 255–98.

83   *There's some kind of link . . . God forgives me:* I am indebted to the teaching of Dr. Tim Keller for insights along these lines. You can order tapes or download MP3s of his messages at www.redeemer.com.

87   *You will seek me and find me when you seek me with all your heart:* See Jeremiah 29:13.

Amidst Weights and Treadmills at the Gym

A Debate About the Age-Old Topic—Sex

DANA BENSON THOUGHT HE'D SET FOOT IN A church for the last time on that humid August morning. That was two days before he would head off to college. He'd had it. How could he ever go back and listen to any preacher as ignorant as the one he'd just heard? Ignorance of other subjects could be overlooked. But such disdain for literature—the growing love of Dana's life—was inexcusable, especially for someone who based his preaching on a book, supposedly the greatest book ever written—the Bible.

That fateful morning, Pastor Liken had begun his sermon trying to relate to the "average" congregants sitting in the pews. He recounted how boring high school English class had been, how little of the required reading he actually read, and how impossible it was to understand anything Charles Dickens took so long to say. How that related to the upcoming sermon escaped Dana.

As he and his father hashed it out in the parking lot, the pitch of the budding literature student's voice rose as he swore he'd never go back to this church or any such place that insulted his intelligence.

"How am I supposed to trust that idiot's interpretation of the Bible if he can't even understand Dickens? How's he supposed to make sense of Hebrew or Greek if he can't read English?"

Richard Benson, no intellectual lightweight himself, had to concede the point to his son. Feeling backed into a corner, he took the risk of giving Dana blanket permission to walk away from their family's faith.

He nodded approval with a reluctant but confident amount of pride, and softly told his son, "I'm glad you're such a good thinker, Dana. God has really given you a great mind. Maybe we can find a church where they value both the Bible and literature and all the other intellectual things you like so much."

"Good luck," was all the soon-to-be freshman could say as he got into their family car and slammed the door behind him.

That was seven years ago. Dana left for college and immersed himself in the academic pleasures of an Ivy League education. His focus on comparative literature was only one of the many intellectual pursuits that captured his heart. In the middle of his junior year, he discovered Dostoyevsky and gobbled up *Crime and Punishment, The Brothers Karamazov,* and *The Idiot,* all before spring break.

Literature may have filled Dana's undergraduate days, but it was women that occupied his evenings—and nights. The liberating world of romantic and existential literature gave Dana the permission his libido craved to discover the intoxicating world of sex. In his freshman year, that craving indulged itself in an intellectual variety of literary pornography. Sophomore year, he found many female classmates willing to share one-night stands with him. Somewhere in the midst of his junior year, a steady girlfriend became his regular sex partner on weekends while his roommate went home to sleep with his fiancé. The summer after graduating, Dana even signed an apartment lease with the woman who had shared his senior-year bed. But after a summer of cohabitation, that relationship came to an ugly end, right as graduate school began.

Now, halfway through his doctoral program, Dostoyevksy, that great Russian novelist, was the focus of all of Dana's waking moments. His committee had just approved the topic for his dissertation. To most people who asked about his topic, Dana would only say, ". . . something about how Dostoyevsky views morality." The focus was, of course, far more precise, but most people's eyes glazed over whenever he talked about it.

Friends closest to Dana couldn't help but notice that these past three years for him were celibate. It wasn't as if he'd stopped dating women—he just stopped sleeping with them.

Larry Wingate, a fellow PhD candidate and exercise partner, knows Dana better than most people around the university. But Dana's moral convictions remain a puzzle to Larry, who sees nothing wrong with consensual, unmarried sex. Larry also studies literature but focuses on American poets. They both value their conversations for their honesty, depth, and humor.

In the midst of the loud music and clanging barbells in Turnerville's Metro Fitness Club, updates about each other's social life fill the time between reps.

❖

LARRY: So, tonight's the big night, huh?

DANA: What do you mean?

LARRY: Aren't you going out with someone tonight? Catherine, I think you said?

DANA: Kathleen. Yeah, we're going to a new film she's been wanting to see.

LARRY: Isn't this the crucial third date?

DANA: It's the third date, but how is that crucial?

LARRY: You know. By the third date, most people are hitting the sheets.

DANA: Oh, yeah. "The third date." I didn't know that was still so standard. Well, we won't be having sex tonight.

LARRY: How can you be so sure? Don't be so negative!

DANA: I'm not being negative, Larry. We already talked about it. Kathleen and I think the same way about sex.

LARRY: Are you kidding me? You talked about this already, after only two dates?

DANA: Let me get this straight. You're surprised that we've *talked* about sex already but you wouldn't be surprised if we've *had* sex already?

LARRY:	Yes. Although, the way you put it does make it sound a bit weird.
DANA:	You think?
LARRY:	I don't know. I do think it's amazing that both of you think sex is taboo.
DANA:	Who said that?
LARRY:	Look, you're not hooking up tonight, right? So you think sex is dirty or something.
DANA:	Just the opposite.
LARRY:	What are you talking about?
DANA:	You think we're not sleeping together because we think sex is bad?
LARRY:	Why else?
DANA:	Maybe because we think it's good!
LARRY:	I'm not following.
DANA:	Listen. Do you think you'll ever get married?
LARRY:	Yeah. What's that got to do with it?
DANA:	You plan to stay faithful to your wife?
LARRY:	Yeah.
DANA:	And you expect her to stay faithful to you?
LARRY:	Yeah.
DANA:	Why?
LARRY:	Why do I want my wife to be faithful to me?
DANA:	Exactly.
LARRY:	I don't want my wife cheating on me. Adultery is wrong. That's why.
DANA:	Why? What's so bad about adultery?
LARRY:	Are you for real?
DANA:	Very. You seem to have no qualms about sleeping with women you're not married to now.
LARRY:	That's different. I've made no commitments to anyone yet. I'm not married, so it doesn't hurt anyone if I have sex.
DANA:	Really?
LARRY:	Really. I can't believe you're such a Puritan. What

	happened to you? You used to hook up with girls when you were an undergrad. Have you now graduated from sex?
DANA:	It might take me awhile to explain. I'm not so sure this is the time or place.
LARRY:	You could start.
DANA:	My decision to stop hooking up had nothing to do with graduating. It's not an undergrad-grad thing.
LARRY:	You just became a Puritan, that's all.
DANA:	What have you got against the Puritans? You know, they weren't as bad as people make them out to be. The Puritans weren't puritanical.
LARRY:	Let's not get into a history debate.
DANA:	Fine. But don't assume all the bad press about the Puritans is accurate. Anyway, my switch was related to some religious convictions.
LARRY:	I knew it. That Christianity stuff will really mess up your sex life.
DANA:	How would you know?
LARRY:	Just look at *you*. You're telling me that now you've got religion, you're not getting any. I rest my case.
DANA:	So lots of sex means good sex?
LARRY:	It sure beats sleeping alone.
DANA:	You never answered my question. What's so bad about adultery?
LARRY:	It hurts people. I already said that.
DANA:	Why does it hurt people?
LARRY:	What are you, in law school? All these questions.
DANA:	C'mon. How does adultery hurt people?
LARRY:	It betrays a trust. When you get married, you're telling your spouse you won't sleep around.
DANA:	All right. You're not seeing my point so I'll just say it. I think the reason adultery is wrong is the same reason that any kind of sex outside marriage is wrong—before or during. Your sleeping around

before marriage is harmful for the same reason that
sleeping around during marriage is wrong.

LARRY: Harmful to who?

DANA: Obviously, it's harmful to the cheated-on spouse, if
          you're married. But I'm saying it's also harmful to
          you, the one who's sleeping around—married or not.

LARRY: How so?

DANA: Because of what sex is—or what sex does. It's
          powerful stuff. It unites two people in an amazing
          way. So if you have sex with someone, it's like you've
          become a part of them and they've become a part
          of you. And I think that's the same, whether you're
          married or not.

LARRY: Sometimes.

DANA: What do you mean?

LARRY: Some sex is that good. But some of it is just so-so.

DANA: And yet you've always bragged to me about every
          single babe you've slept with. You remember every
          single one of them. I'm not talking about the physical
          experience—like whether your orgasms were
          simultaneous. It's something deeper than that. Every
          sexual encounter has had a big effect on you.

LARRY: You're dreaming. Premarital sex just doesn't have the
          stigma it once had.

DANA: Did you marry any of those women?

LARRY: Of course not.

DANA: Then it wasn't really *premarital*, was it?

LARRY: Technically . . . no.

DANA: Technically, it was extramarital sex.

LARRY: What's the big deal?

DANA: It was something you were willing to do with your
          body but not with your soul.

LARRY: How quaint.

DANA: I'm serious. Don't you see that your so-called casual
          sex has been anything but casual?

LARRY: No, I don't.

DANA: You want it both ways, don't you? You want sex to
              be the biggest thing in the world—that's why you're
              always talking about it. But you also want it to be just
              a casual fling so you can dismiss it. Which is it?

LARRY: I'm not always talking about it.

DANA: What I'm trying to say is that there's a reason it's
              called "adultery." It adulterates a relationship. It adds
              something that makes it less than pure. And I'm
              also saying that when you have sex with someone
              you're not committed to, it adulterates *you*. It does
              something to *you* that's bad for you. It fragments
              you.

LARRY: What century are you living in? Not all sex is that
              meaningful.

DANA: Oh, I realize what I'm saying is ridiculously out of
              step with our world. Most people would think I'm
              insane if they heard me.

LARRY: Maybe just a little.

DANA: But I can't find a middle ground. Either sex is what
              the Bible says it is or it's just a physical act like dogs
              do. If the way sex is shown on TV is right, then what's
              the big deal? It doesn't matter how many people you
              have sex with. If the Bible's right . . . Oh, I'm repeating
              myself. Eh . . . maybe you're right.

LARRY: What?

DANA: For you, sex isn't always a big deal. But you know
              what. I think that's terrible. That's part of why I
              decided to quit having sex until I get married.

LARRY: I don't follow.

DANA: Sex got to the point where it wasn't all that
              meaningful for me, either. Jeannette and I had sex
              all through our senior year. We lived together. But
              instead of sex being more meaningful to us, it actually
              became passionless.

LARRY: Well, you've got to try different things, different
             positions, you know.

DANA: Hey, we tried plenty of things. Physically it was
             fine. It's just that our relationship lacked any kind
             of meaning. We were just roommates who had sex.
             Instead of it binding us together, it was a wedge
             between us.

LARRY: So she wasn't the right one.

DANA: It's more than that. We decided to live together
             because we wanted to see if we should get married.
             We bought the whole line that you have to live
             together in order to find out if you're compatible.

LARRY: You sound kind of condescending.

DANA: I am. That's just a bunch of garbage. My parents never
             lived together before they got married. They didn't
             sleep together either. But somehow that hasn't hurt
             them in their forty-three years of staying tight.

LARRY: That was a long time ago. Our whole culture has
             changed.

DANA: That's for sure. But biology hasn't changed. I'm sure
             my parents were just as hot for each other as anyone
             today—maybe more. But I think, for them, not living
             together was what helped them stay married all these
             years.

LARRY: How so?

DANA: When Jeannette and I moved in together, what we
             were actually saying was, "If we don't like this, we'll
             break up. We can have sex. We can live together. We
             just don't have to commit." But when my parents got
             married, they were saying, "Once we move in together
             and have sex, there's no turning back." It's almost as if
             Jeannette and I guaranteed we wouldn't stay together
             and my parents guaranteed that they would.

LARRY: You're making less and less sense to me. Maybe you're
             lifting too much weight.

DANA: Hey—do some research. Couples who sleep together
           and live together before they get married are far more
           likely to get divorced. Their marriages break up more
           often than people who say they won't sleep together
           until they exchange rings.

LARRY: Where are you getting this from?

DANA: You can find the research in a lot of places. And it's
           not just in Puritan journals! And the same research
           says premarital sex actually leads to extramarital sex.

LARRY: But your parents got married way before the whole
           sexual revolution. I mean *Playboy* magazine wasn't
           even around when they got married.

DANA: Now there's a great cultural icon—Hugh Hefner.
           What a great American he is!

LARRY: You know, they did a whole bio of him on the History
           channel the other night. You should've seen it.

DANA: I don't doubt that he had an effect on history. I'm just
           saying it may not have been a positive effect.

LARRY: What's so bad about helping people get unrepressed?

DANA: Is that what he did?

LARRY: You do have to admit that our society had been
           repressed sexually. And the Christian church sure had
           a lot to do with it.

DANA: The church doesn't have the greatest track record
           about sex. I'll grant you that. That's part of why I
           left it when I started as an undergrad. But the two
           extremes—the repressive church and the exploitative
           Hefner—are both unhealthy. I'm looking for another
           alternative.

LARRY: You think Hefner is exploitative?

DANA: You amaze me sometimes. What's your niece's
           name—the one you're always talking about?

LARRY: Colleen. What's she got to do with it?

DANA: How old is she?

LARRY: Five. Your point?

DANA:	Do you hope she grows up to be a porn star?
LARRY:	She'd make a ton of money.
DANA:	And have millions of guys lusting after her. Answer my question. You want Colleen to be the babe guys talk about in the locker room?
LARRY:	I don't know.
DANA:	Oh, c'mon, Larry. Be real. Would her parents be proud if she were the star of the latest porn video being downloaded around the world? Would you brag that she's made it to Hefner's five-hot-babes list? You know, the ones he takes turns sleeping with, after popping his latest dose of Viagra.
LARRY:	Hey, keep your voice down. People are beginning to look at you.
DANA:	What's the big deal, Larry? Sex is okay, right? Why the need to keep it hushed up? You're not one of those repressive Puritans, are you?
LARRY:	You need a shower, man. A cold one.
DANA:	You really aren't understanding me. I actually do feel weird talking about this here, with all these people around. Do you think that . . . maybe . . . sex is supposed to be a private thing? I could explain this better, I think, if we were outside.
LARRY:	Let's go get something to drink. We can talk outside on one of those benches.
DANA:	Deal.

❖

Later. Showered. Outside. Private.

❖

LARRY:	I trust that your shower was sufficiently cold enough to calm you down. You really got crazy in there.

DANA: That's funny. I'm the crazy one?

LARRY: I'm not saying you're crazy. You were just *acting* a
             little crazy, that's all.

DANA: Well, these are crazy times. There's more explicit talk
             about sex, but it seems that people are more miserable
             about sex than ever.

LARRY: Miserable?

DANA: Frustrated. Fearful. Abusive. All of the above.

LARRY: Why don't you back up and tell me what made you
             change your views. How did religion change your
             sleeping habits?

DANA: Well, after Jeannette broke up with me—

LARRY: Wait a minute. She broke up with you? I thought it
             was the other way around.

DANA: No. She ended it and moved out.

LARRY: How come?

DANA: She accused me of cheating on her.

LARRY: Why would she do that?

DANA: Because I was.

LARRY: Whoa!

DANA: Yeah. Whoa is right. I was like an animal. I was out
             of control. I think I was also scared. This was the
             first relationship that was anything more than just
             adolescent lust. And I think it was more than I could
             handle. So . . . I bailed rather than committing.

LARRY: Didn't you apologize?

DANA: Kinda. It was a crazy thing, Larry. I had such
             conflicting things inside me. On the one hand, I knew
             she was right—that we had a kind of commitment
             that I shouldn't have violated but, on the other
             hand—

LARRY: What other hand? She was right to get mad at you.

DANA: Was she? I mean, we weren't married. We were just
             living together.

LARRY: Didn't that mean that you wouldn't cheat on her?

DANA: Yes and no—it does and it doesn't. That's the problem
          with moving in together. What does it really mean?
          It means we were willing to sleep together without a
          lifelong commitment. How is that so different from
          sleeping with someone else whom I didn't have a
          lifelong commitment with?

LARRY: Well . . . to be honest, I'm not sure.

DANA: Bingo. That's exactly the tension I faced. It was like all
          of a sudden my whole philosophy of relationships was
          staring me in the face. It was a big sham.

LARRY: Are you sure you're not overreacting?

DANA: At the time, I was just confused. You're hearing
          me say all this after years of processing it. But no,
          I don't think I'm overreacting. I had a real inner
          contradiction going on. I wanted sex to be binding
          and unbinding at the same time. It just won't work
          that way.

LARRY: So what happened after you got over being dumped?

DANA: I don't know if I'll ever get over it.

LARRY: Really? It's been like three years!

DANA: I don't know if this'll make sense to you. My change
          in thinking about sex and relationships was all bound
          up in my change in thinking about God. Are you sure
          you're up for listening to my whole deal?

LARRY: Give it a try. If I think you're preaching too much, I'll
          tell you.

DANA: Good. You know that I grew up going to church all
          the time. And that my family's pretty active in their
          church.

LARRY: Right. And . . . as I seem to recall, it wasn't all that
          great of an experience for you.

DANA: Not the whole thing. It was just at the end of high
          school that I got sick of that church's particular brand
          of ignorant Christianity.

LARRY: I remember you telling me about all that.

DANA: So when Jeannette broke up with me, I felt like my
           world got rocked, and I needed some kind of stability
           again. It's a long story but I ended up going back to
           church.

LARRY: That same one in your hometown?

DANA: No, not at all. Up here near campus. I found a very
           different kind of church.

LARRY: Like a different denomination?

DANA: It's not a denomination thing. They're both
           independent churches. But the flavor of this one up
           here is completely different. It's more thoughtful and
           . . . I don't know . . . less reactionary. It fits more with
           a campus-type environment.

LARRY: One of those more liberal churches?

DANA: No. It's not a matter of conservative or liberal. This
           one's theology is conservative but it allows for deeper
           discussion than most churches—conservative or
           liberal.

LARRY: So, you like . . . got born-again again?

DANA: Not exactly. But I did rediscover my faith. Maybe I
           became a Christian for the first time. It's hard to say.
           That's another discussion.

LARRY: Yeah. Go back to the stuff about relationships.

DANA: It's hard to separate the God things from the sex
           things.

LARRY: I'll bet no one in the history of the world has ever said
           what you just said.

DANA: Ha! That's funny. But maybe not. I started seeing—
           remember, now, what I'm saying is like three years
           worth of thinking and wrestling with this—it was
           like I saw God differently. I was realizing that he's the
           one who created us and created sex, so he's got the
           right to say what's okay and what's not okay.

LARRY: I'm beginning to sense a sermon coming on.

DANA: Not really. But I started understanding that line,

"There is no virtue if there is no immortality." Or maybe, in my case, it was, "If God is irrelevant, than anything is allowable."

LARRY: Go on.

DANA: God's the one who came up with the idea of sex, and that whole thing about the two becoming one flesh is how he designed it. But, for years, I was living by a different set of rules about sex—and it just can't work that way.

LARRY: You keep saying that—"it just can't work that way." Why not?

DANA: Why can't fish fly?

LARRY: Huh?

DANA: It's not what they're built for! People are not made to be compartmentalized animals.

LARRY: Dana, I'm really trying to follow you on this. But I'm not getting it.

DANA: Maybe it just doesn't make sense unless you're a Christian. I don't know.

LARRY: Oh, c'mon. That can't be right. If what you believe is right, it should make sense even to people like me, who don't buy the whole religious part.

DANA: Maybe. But this isn't just an intellectual thing—it's a moral thing. So I don't know if these ideas will make any sense to you.

LARRY: Well, let's keep trying. Assume it can.

DANA: All right. Here's what I'm trying to say. God designed sex to be an all-encompassing, total-person glue— only two people, for a whole lifetime. I was trying to make sex something else—some nice, fun, quasi-meaningful thing but not a whole-person, whole-life thing.

LARRY: That's why you said what you did about your parents.

DANA: Right. For them, it's something that's taking a whole lifetime to perfect. But they seem to be doing pretty

LARRY: well at it. If marriage were, say, a car, sex for them is like the motor. But other parts of the car are really important too.

LARRY: Like what?

DANA: Communication, common goals, friendship. Stuff like that.

LARRY: Okay.

DANA: Marriage needs sex, like a car needs a motor, but it needs other things too. I think marriage makes two people more stable, more secure, more healed from their past. It makes them more whole.

LARRY: I'm still stuck with why that can't happen with just living together.

DANA: Because the very essence of living together is fragmentation. It divides people—no, it disintegrates them.

LARRY: Another overstatement?

DANA: I don't think so. Think about it. Disintegrate. Dis-integrity. It destroys integrity or wholeness, or whatever you want to call it. You compartmentalize sex and, before you know it, you're a fragmented person. That's what was happening to me. You're saying to your partner, "I'll give you my body but not my whole life." So I have to divorce my physical life from the other parts of my life. It was driving me crazy.

LARRY: Like how?

DANA: My capacity to care—about anybody or anything—was just crashing. I was becoming really selfish. That's why I cheated on Jeannette. I wanted sex in some kind of impersonal, detached way, and I couldn't do that with Jeannette anymore. I knew her too well. We were becoming one in more ways than just physical. I was so used to sex as an impersonal thing that I actually preferred the non-intimacy kind of sex to the real thing.

LARRY: You're sounding like a Dostoyevsky character.

DANA: So be it. Maybe I am a bit like Raskolnikov. But I'd rather be like I am now, even though I'm not having any sex, than the way I was before.

LARRY: So you're kind of in a sexual Siberia.

DANA: Very good.

LARRY: And you talked about all this with Kathleen on the second date?

DANA: Not as in depth as this. We just found out that we've both got Christian convictions about sex, and we're assuming we're on the same page about the details. We've talked enough to know that we've both tried it *our* way and that the Christian way is better.

LARRY: She lived with someone?

DANA: Yeah. For two years! But they broke up too.

LARRY: And you're okay with that?

DANA: Ha! That's interesting that you should wonder about that. But that's the other part of the Christian thing. Not only is God the one with the authority to say what's right, he's also the one who forgives.

LARRY: That sounds nice . . . but it doesn't sound all that romantic.

DANA: Maybe not. Romance may be part of the problem.

LARRY: You're a literature major and you're down on romance?

DANA: Hear me out. Romance is nice. Kathleen and I are going out for dinner before the movie tonight. It'll be romantic. I'm looking forward to it. Yes. Yes. Yes.

LARRY: But . . .

DANA: But romance, as an end in itself, is a dead end.

LARRY: It's not an end in itself—sex is the goal, remember?

DANA: Be serious. The problem with romance—and you *can* include sex with it—is that it makes the relationship the highest value.

LARRY: What should be higher?

DANA: God—the One who made us relational people, the
           One who gave us sex as a gift, the One who should
           be our focus. Relationships can't take the pressure if
           they're the central focus of our lives.

LARRY: But you're the one saying that marriage is so
           important.

DANA: It's very important. It's just not the highest
           importance.

LARRY: What do you mean . . . how did you say it? . . .
           romance can't take the pressure?

DANA: Overemphasizing romance came as part of the enlight-
           enment. People had given up on God and put man in
           his place. We worshiped ourselves and what we could
           do, instead of worshiping God and what he's done.

LARRY: I'm familiar with this. It's the theory that we must
           worship something and if it isn't God, it'll be
           ourselves or something else.

DANA: You got it. Sex is a frequent replacement as something
           to worship. Ever notice how many times beautiful
           women are called, "sex goddesses"?

LARRY: Interesting.

DANA: So we started worshiping ourselves—or our
           relationships—instead of God. But people can't
           satisfy our need to worship.

LARRY: You know, I hate to say it—but I think that's what
           happened to my parents. Or at least to my dad. He
           worshiped my mom but then, all of a sudden, he left
           her when she wasn't satisfying anymore. And now
           he's with wife number three. And she's probably a
           disappointment.

DANA: That's got to be hard for you to watch.

LARRY: It still is—even after all these years.

DANA: You're not alone. They say the effects of divorce never
           totally subside. Somehow the notion of "easy divorce"
           never became as easy as they said.

LARRY:	But what you're saying about marriage is making some sense.
DANA:	Good.
LARRY:	But I don't see the enlightenment kind of romance still being in vogue. Don't you think we've seen that it doesn't work?
DANA.	Yes we have. But look what we've replaced it with. Cold realism, cynicism, despair. Romance is out, but so is any kind of hope.
LARRY:	You're right. I certainly see it in a lot of poetry that I'm studying.
DANA:	And music. And theater. And art. It's like we went from worshiping God, to worshiping ourselves, to worshiping nothing— and it's left us pretty depressed and hopeless.
LARRY:	So what do you propose?
DANA:	Redemptive love.
LARRY:	Hey, nice alliteration—Romanticism, Realism, Redemption.
DANA:	I didn't plan it that way. Anyway, we shouldn't worship relationships but we shouldn't give up on them either. We should worship God and accept relationships as gifts from him to be used as part of his redeeming us.
LARRY:	That's good. You ought to write this down.
DANA:	I'm a little busy writing something else right now.
LARRY:	Oh, yeah . . . your doctoral thesis. Me too. Which means I better get going.
DANA:	Hey, wait a minute. You see that couple right over there—crossing the parking lot?
LARRY:	The old ones?
DANA:	Yeah. Karl and Louise. They live down the street from me. He just turned eighty. I think she's like . . . seventy-eight. They've been married for fifty-four years. She invited all the neighbors to a party she threw for him for his eightieth birthday.

LARRY: Hope it wasn't a surprise party.

DANA: Ha! No. Too risky.

LARRY: Exactly.

DANA: But, here's the deal. They're crazy about each other.
            You should have seen them at the party. It was like
            they were reaping all the benefits of fifty-plus years of
            staying together.

LARRY: And you're saying that it's all right that it's not so
            romantic.

DANA: In a sense, it's incredibly romantic—just not like the
            crazy stuff you see on the reality shows. Doesn't it
            make you gag when people who've known each other
            for like . . . a week . . . start talking about being soul
            mates? Karl and Louise know a ton more about being
            soul mates.

LARRY: But they wouldn't make for very good TV.

DANA: Right. But so what? I'd trade the heat and passion
            of TV sex any day for the kind of tightness Karl and
            Louise have.

LARRY: Yeah. If you're lucky.

DANA: I think luck's got less to do with it than you think. I
            think it's a lot more of trading one kind of pleasure
            for another.

LARRY: How so?

DANA: Trading the short-term hooking up pleasure for the
            long-term stability pleasure. I don't think you can
            have both. So I'm making the bet that the security
            thing is its own kind of pleasure. It sure looked that
            way on Karl's face when he kissed his wife on his
            eightieth birthday.

LARRY: It's a gamble though. Some couples their age are
            miserable.

DANA: You're right. But I'm willing to take the chance. I want
            the woman who I marry when I'm thirty to be the
            same one who throws a party for me when I'm eighty.

LARRY:	And everything in between? Sounds kind of boring.
DANA:	That kind of boring I can take! The same hand you hold today, just walking down the street, is the one you'll be holding when you're eighty—and the doctor tells you you've got cancer. If you call that boring, I don't know what to tell you.
LARRY:	I didn't really mean boring. I'm not sure what I meant.
DANA:	It's hard to think about relationships in categories after all we've been flooded with in the media.
LARRY:	Yeah. But it's worth considering.
DANA:	People think Christians have too low a view of sex. And that's true for a lot of Christians. But I think it's just the opposite. We think very highly of sex—but we give sex the proper place in our lives. It's ironic, isn't it? You put sex on too high a pedestal, and it ends up meaning practically nothing. You keep it in its rightful place, and it ends up meaning a lot.
LARRY:	Is this going to be part of your dissertation?
DANA:	I doubt it.
LARRY:	It should.
DANA:	Hey . . . you said you needed to go. Sorry I've talked too long.
LARRY:	That's all right. See you Wednesday?
DANA:	Yeah.

❖

Keep the Conversation Going

- Proverbs 5–7 would provide a theoretical backdrop for the Christian view of marriage and sex presented in this chapter.
- Philip Yancey's *Rumors of Another World: What on Earth Are We Missing?* (Grand Rapids: Zondervan, 2003), argues that

sex is a kind of evidence for God's existence and goodness. See, especially, chapter 5, "Designer Sex," 73–96.

98   *Hey—do some research*: One source would be Linda J. Waite and Maggie Gallagher, *The Case for Marriage: Why Married People Are Happier, Healthier, and Better Off Financially* (New York: Doubleday, 2000).

103   *There is no virtue if there is no immortality*: Fyodor Dostoyevsky, *The Brothers Karamazov* (New York: Farrar, Straus and Giroux, 1990), 70. An intriguing discussion of the work of Dostoyevsky in the formation of Christian belief can be found in Philip Yancey's *Soul Survivor: How Thirteen Unlikely Mentors Helped My Faith Survive the Church* (New York: Galilee Trade, 2003), 119–46.

      God's the one who came up with the idea of sex, and that whole thing about the two becoming one flesh: See Genesis 2:24.

106   *Overemphasizing romance came as part of the enlightenment. People had given up on God and put man in his place*: See Paul Johnson, *Intellectuals* (New York: Harper and Row, 1988), for some painful displays of this theory.

      They say the effects of divorce never totally subside: Judith Wallerstein, Julia Lewis, and Sandra Blakeslee, *The Unexpected Legacy of Divorce: A 25-Year Landmark Study* (New York: Hyperion, 2000).

107   *And music. And theater. And art*: Despite some dated examples, see Francis A. Schaeffer, *Escape from Reason* (Downers Grove, Ill.: InterVarsity, 1968).

Near AJ's, Turnerville's Upscale Gay Bar

An Unusual Chat Between Two Friends

AJ's, AT THE CORNER OF KIRCH AND MADISON STREETS, serves up the best Reuben in the county. So it's understandable that the lunchtime crowd keeps the place buzzing from 11:30 until almost 3:00. But after dark, the clientele changes dramatically. With the draw of great music, a large dance floor, and a well-stocked bar, AJ's is the place to be—if you're gay.

This no longer bothers the people of Turnerville. Everybody knows now what most people used to only suspect. Turnerville didn't turn gay friendly by legislative fiat, or with scientific discoveries, or from well-reasoned arguments. Like the rest of America, people came to accept homosexuality by watching sit-coms, laughing at gay jokes, and by sympathizing with a persecuted minority. Image, not substance, predisposed people to overcome distaste for this "alternative lifestyle."

The brutal murder of Matthew Shepherd in 1998 reinforced for most of Turnerville's residents their acceptance of gays. Laramie, Wyoming, shares many cultural and demographic similarities with Turnerville. As the newspapers unveiled the gruesome details of the murder of that young, gay man, people frequently commented, "It could have happened just as easily right here!"

When Donnie Stone and Ed Denson bump into each other across

the street from AJ's, they have no idea what kind of conversation lies in store for them. When they were fresh out of college, they worked for the Turnerville Dispatch—Donnie in the newsroom, Ed as a sportswriter. They saw each other daily, shared quite a few lunches, and discussed politics, sports, and swapped the latest joke. Now, both in their mid-thirties and not having seen each other in almost ten years, they have a lot of catching up to do.

ED: Whoa! Donnie? Donnie Stone? Is that you?

DONNIE: Yeah. Ed? Wow. What are you doing back in Turnerville?

ED: Actually, I don't live that far away. I'm just back for an eye doctor's appointment. You don't still live near here, do you?

DONNIE: Nah. I was in the area doing an interview for a radio station and I just thought I'd come by and see the old neighborhood. Still a great town, isn't it?

ED: Sure is. So you've switched from print to radio, huh?

DONNIE: Kind of. What are you up to? Are you married?

ED: Yep. Married. Two kids. A mini-van. The whole suburban deal. I'm still writing, for the *Tribune*.

DONNIE: Moving up in the world of journalism. That's great. Say, do you have lunch plans?

ED: No, I don't. That would be great. Why don't we go to AJ's?

DONNIE: Well . . . do we have any other choices?

ED: There's fast food out on highway six. AJ's is a lot nicer.

DONNIE: Isn't there that diner down on Short Street?

ED: Yeah. That's a good place. Sure. It's quieter in there, I think. We can actually walk there.

DONNIE: Great. Let's go. You have two kids, eh? How old are they?

ED: Seven and five. Two daughters. I get to pay for college *and* the weddings! My financial planner loves me. How about you? Married? Kids?

DONNIE: I actually just got married two years ago. And we've got a new baby girl, Maria. Just four months old.

ED: That's great! Are you getting any sleep yet?

DONNIE: Just barely. So if I'm falling asleep over lunch, don't wake me.

ED: I remember those days. Just got married, huh? You sure waited a while. Hey, here's the diner. Why don't you get us a table? I need to use the men's room.

DONNIE: Sure.

A few minutes later, after ordering their meals.

ED: Donnie, this may be totally out of line. But . . . it seemed like you were really uncomfortable with the possibility of eating lunch at AJ's. You've heard that they've finally come out of the closet, haven't you? I mean, that everyone now knows it's a gay bar at night. And everyone's cool about it. . . . But you didn't seem so cool.

DONNIE: I'd heard that. Most people probably knew about the nighttime scene there for quite a while before it became official.

ED: Especially with the Matthew Shepherd thing. There was a whole candlelight vigil held right outside AJ's front door. That was like . . . eight years ago, already?

DONNIE: Has it been that long?

ED: I think so. Ever since then, there's no pretense. And I think that's the way it should be.

DONNIE: I actually saw that candlelight vigil on the news.

ED: So what's the deal with you? You aren't homophobic,
           are you?

DONNIE: That's a great word, isn't it?

ED: Homophobic?

DONNIE: Yeah. There aren't too many words like it. You just say
           it and you've already branded anyone who disagrees
           with you as psychologically disturbed.

ED: What? Are you saying that it's okay to hate gays?

DONNIE: Are those my only options? Hatred or acceptance?

ED: What other option would you like?

DONNIE: Several. Look, I'm just saying that maybe this issue isn't
           quite so simple.

ED: How?

DONNIE: If you watch TV, you get the idea you can see things
           only one of two ways. Either people are born gay and
           that's all there is to it. Or you're a bigot and you hate
           gays the way the Ku Klux Klan hates blacks.

ED: You think people aren't born gay?

DONNIE: I think being gay isn't good.

ED: How can you even use words like *good* or *bad*? Being
           gay just is.

DONNIE: How do you know that?

ED: Look, I've got gay friends. I even have a cousin who's
           a lesbian. They're not perverts. They're just gay. That's
           the way they were born. They didn't choose it.

DONNIE: I agree with you that they probably didn't choose it.

ED: So what's the big deal?

DONNIE: I realize that I'm saying some things that are way out of
           touch with where our society is. But I've done a lot of
           thinking and reading about this. A lot. I've got plenty
           of gay friends, too. I just think there's a whole side to
           this topic that most people never even imagine.

ED: Like what?

DONNIE: Like some people change. They see being gay as some-
           thing that's more like a problem than a God-given trait.

ED:	Change? From being gay to being straight?
DONNIE:	Yeah.
ED:	And I suppose you believe in unicorns too.
DONNIE:	I told you this is 180 degrees from where our society is. But I'm pretty convinced that a lot of gays don't have to stay that way. In fact, a lot of gay people would really love to change.
ED:	That's just because there are a lot of hateful jerks out there.
DONNIE:	I think it's a lot deeper than that. Being gay is a problem.
ED:	I can't believe you. You sound so judgmental. Haven't you ever heard, "Judge not, lest you be judged?"
DONNIE:	Yes. I've heard that. Jesus said it.
ED:	So where do you get off telling these people their sexual orientation is some kind of problem?
DONNIE:	There's *another* great vocabulary change—*sexual orientation*. Remember when the term used to be *sexual preference*?
ED:	Yeah. But people realized it wasn't a preference. Just like you didn't "prefer" to have white skin.
DONNIE:	Hey. I'm sorry. I didn't think this is where our lunch was going. This isn't turning out to be all that great of a reunion.
ED:	It's okay. I'd like to keep talking about this because I really don't get what you're trying to say. You're sounding like some kind of fundamentalist, right-wing Christian. But that doesn't fit with who you used to be. Did you have some kind of personality change or something?
DONNIE:	Wow. That's a really long story. Have you got six hours?
ED:	No. But I'd like to hear some of it. I can't figure out how you became so judgmental.
DONNIE:	All right. Let's tackle that one. The bit about "Judge not." What do you think "Judge not, lest you be judged" means?

ED: Just what it says. No one has the right to tell anyone
           that they're wrong about the way they live.

DONNIE: Really? You think that's what it means?

ED: Yeah.

DONNIE: That sounds impossible to do.

ED: Why?

DONNIE: 'Cause it sounds so judgmental.

ED: How do you mean?

DONNIE: If no one's ever supposed to tell anyone that they're
           wrong, you just broke that rule. You're telling *me* that
           I'm wrong for judging.

ED: Say that again.

DONNIE: I say being gay is bad. So that's judging, right?

ED: Right.

DONNIE: Then you tell me I'm wrong for saying that. So that's
           judging, too. We're both judging.

ED: Hmm.

DONNIE: And Jesus was judging when he told people not to
           judge!—and when he called people hypocrites. And
           lots of other times. He broke his own rule—if that's
           what judging is.

ED: Hey. He's Jesus. He can do whatever he wants. It's okay
           for him to make those kinds of . . . uh . . .

DONNIE: Judgments?

ED: I guess.

DONNIE: But he also told his followers some things that require
           them to make those kinds of evaluations. I think that's
           a better word.

ED: What kind of evaluations?

DONNIE: He told his followers to watch out for dogs—that's a
           pretty harsh word. He told them to beware of wolves in
           sheep's clothing. He warned his followers to stay away
           from people who are trying to mess them up. We have
           to make those kinds of evaluations all the time.

ED: So what did he mean by "Judge not"?

DONNIE: He meant, "Don't condemn"—don't put people down
            in insulting, degrading ways. People deserve respect,
            even if they're doing some really bad things. That
            doesn't mean we can't evaluate and say that some
            things people are *doing* are wrong. If you sat here and
            told me you were a child molester, I wouldn't say,
            "Well, hey, who am I to judge?"

ED: You really *have* done a lot of thinking about this.

DONNIE: More than you'd ever believe.

ED: Why? What prompted all this?

DONNIE: You talked about Matthew Shepherd's murder.
            That was a big event for me—the whole way the gay
            community reacted, the way they told reporters how to
            cover the story.

ED: I remember. There were all those briefing sessions by
            gay leaders. It was 'cause we were all so unaccustomed
            to writing about their world.

DONNIE: Maybe. I think they had other motivations.

ED: Like what?

DONNIE: Have you ever heard of Jesse Dirkhising?

ED: No. Not at all.

DONNIE: I didn't think so. Nobody has. Everybody in the world
            has heard of Matthew Shepherd but nobody's heard of
            Jesse.

ED: Who is he?

DONNIE: Jesse Dirkhising died almost a year after Matthew
            Shepherd. But how those two stories were covered
            changed my life.

ED: All right. I'm listening.

DONNIE: It's not a very good mealtime topic.

ED: I'll take the risk.

DONNIE: Okay. Jesse Dirkhising was also a young gay boy. He
            was only thirteen, and he, too, was killed in a terrible
            way. But he was killed by two older gay men. I'll spare
            you the disgusting details, but they used him for their

own sexual perversions, drugged him, gagged him
so he wouldn't yell, and put tape over his mouth. He
suffocated.

ED: And you're sparing me the worst of this story?

DONNIE: Believe me. I am.

ED: Well, look. There are all sorts of sickos—gay and
           straight—who rape and abuse. This doesn't prove that
           homosexuality is bad.

DONNIE: No, it doesn't. But compare the way the gay community
           hushed this story up to the way they indoctrinated
           the media about Matthew Shepherd—it shows a side
           to that world that's really sick. Some of them even
           admitted as much in their magazines—but that was a
           lot later. That was the turning point for me. I just had
           to get out.

ED: Of journalism?

DONNIE: No. Look . . . you're getting a lot more than you
           bargained for when I asked you to lunch. I didn't plan
           on this coming up.

ED: Hey, I brought it up. It's fine.

DONNIE: Ed . . . I used to be gay.

ED: Excuse me?

DONNIE: I used to be gay. When I was talking a little while ago
           about people who experience change, I was referring to
           myself—and lots of other people too.

ED: I've heard about people who tried to switch. Didn't
           Seinfeld have an episode about this? But it never lasts.

DONNIE: Is Seinfeld where you get all your facts about being gay?

ED: No. Don't be ridiculous.

DONNIE: Are you sure that television hasn't taught you more
           about homosexuality than any other source?

ED: I think I've learned more from my gay friends.

DONNIE: How much do they really tell you about their world?

ED: That's none of my business.

DONNIE: Fine. Just don't assume you've got all the data you need to make good conclusions. I saw that Seinfeld episode too. All those sitcoms put a good face on being gay. They make it seem it's just like being straight. But don't believe it. I was in the gay world for more than ten years—it's a very corrupt, manipulative world.

ED: Ten years? So you were gay when we worked together?

DONNIE: Yep. I was at AJ's three or four nights a week at one point. Lots of memories. Most of them are pretty painful to me now.

ED: I never would've guessed.

DONNIE: We're very good at presenting a certain kind of image. It's one of our acquired skills. We're also pretty good at stiff-arming.

ED: Stiff-arming?

DONNIE: Keeping people at arm's length—or further—if we want them to know only certain things about us, but not everything.

ED: But you weren't really gay, were you? I mean, how can you be straight now?

DONNIE: You've never heard of this kind of thing?

ED: I don't think so.

DONNIE: There are a lot of us ex-gays. Look up Exodus International on the Internet sometime. You'd be amazed.

ED: I *am* amazed.

DONNIE: The fact that you've never heard of people like me proves my point.

ED: What point?

DONNIE: That you've only heard one side of the story.

ED: Are you sure this is good for you to be married now? I mean—to a woman? I've heard of gay guys marrying women just to make themselves straight. It's like a kind of denial. But it never works.

DONNIE: Never? You've done a sociological study of this?

ED: You know what I mean.

DONNIE: I know that you believe what people have told you to
                      believe.

ED: Indoctrination again? That seems to be a recurring
                      theme for you.

DONNIE: It's the recurring theme of my life these days. I know
                      that some guys try the white-knuckle approach—they
                      hang on to a woman, or they get married, hoping it'll
                      make them straight. I think my case is different. It's
                      been a long process.

ED: You're not worried that you'll wake up one morning
                      and realize you've always been gay and you can't
                      change?

DONNIE: It always amazes me how many people question my
                      heterosexuality more than my homosexuality. Maybe
                      all those gay years were the unhealthy years—the ones
                      of denial. Denying I had some real pain in my life, and
                      I was trying to satisfy it with relationships with men.
                      I think it's very good that I'm married to a woman. I
                      can't believe God brought someone so great into my life
                      after all the things I've done.

ED: So were you just faking it all those years you were gay?

DONNIE: This is really hard for you, isn't it? No. I wasn't
                      faking it. I was desperate, though. I was trying to
                      satisfy a hunger for love and affection. None of those
                      relationships with guys could satisfy it, though. None.
                      And believe me. I had a lot of them.

ED: Ten years. I can't get over this.

DONNIE: I didn't think I ever would either. Most of my
                      relationships were really bad—lots of verbal and
                      emotional abuse. Even some physical abuse.

ED: Really?

DONNIE: You'd be amazed how common it is in gay couples.

ED: You're right. I would be.

DONNIE: You could do tons of research about codependency by studying gay relationships. Each breakup was harder for me than the one before. But none of those relationships ever lasted—because they can't.

ED: Why not?

DONNIE: It's like cotton candy. You're trying to satisfy a real hunger for real food. Cotton candy just can't satisfy. It just keeps you coming back for more.

ED: But some gay guys are in committed, long-term relationships—aren't they?

DONNIE: Yes. They're kind of the exception, though. And be careful how you use the word "long-term." They love to throw that around. I saw Barbra Streisand on Oprah one time, and she said she'd been with her current husband for seven years and people started cheering like she said fifty-seven.

ED: But some gay couples last together a long time.

DONNIE: Right. I know. But that still doesn't make it good. There are reasons why civilizations have rejected homosexuality. And it's not just homophobia. There are just some unhealthy things about the gay world. You can read about it, if you want. I'd rather not spell them out here. I've still got the rest of my lunch to eat.

ED: So, all your relationships ended badly.

DONNIE: Well, not my last one. That actually was a good relationship—as gay things go. But even the best guy in the world can't do what a healthy, godly relationship between a man and a woman can do. I didn't know that at the time, but it's as clear as can be to me now.

ED: What do you mean "a godly relationship"?

DONNIE: I'd become a Christian when I was in junior high. But sometime after that . . . I don't know . . . maybe two or three years later—I don't think I was in high school yet—I had my first gay encounter. This guy in my neighborhood . . . well, I can skip the details. I *will* say, though, looking back at it now, I was taken advantage

ED: of terribly. I'd even call it sexual abuse. But I was really longing for affection, and I was attracted to this guy.

ED: Attracted. You mean physically?

DONNIE: It's hard to describe, but the physical attraction is actually only a part of it. I was drawn by his self-confidence, I guess. Maybe "attracted" is the wrong word, but it was much stronger than admiration. I just wanted to spend more time with him, get close enough to "absorb" the traits I saw in him that I felt so deficient in. Unfortunately, it led to more than I bargained for.

ED: You didn't tell anyone about this?

DONNIE: Are you kidding? It was like I had two conflicting responses—and both of them made it impossible to tell anyone. On the one hand, I felt horrible. I felt used. But on the other hand, I really loved the affection this guy showed me.

ED: It happened more than once?

DONNIE: Oh yes. A lot more.

ED: You started by saying you became a Christian. How does that fit?

DONNIE: It doesn't. That's just it. I knew enough about the Bible to know that what I was doing was wrong. But I just couldn't seem to stay away from this guy—or all the gay porn he showed me.

ED: The Bible does say this is wrong, doesn't it?

DONNIE: Yes. But just knowing that didn't make much of a difference. Later, when I was in college and involved in Bible studies, I checked out those verses to see if they really do say that homosexuality is wrong. They do. But, like I said, that didn't stop me.

ED: And yet there are some churches that say being gay isn't a sin. How do they interpret those verses?

DONNIE: Oh, man. That would take days to discuss. I'll send you a book that looks at all the verses, if you want. I went to one of those churches for a while—I really wanted to make being gay and being Christian fit together. But

they don't fit. Their interpretations of those verses are
almost laughable. Did you know they say that the real
sin of Sodom and Gomorrah wasn't homosexuality? It
was "inhospitality."

ED: That's creative.

DONNIE: I think the Bible's teaching about sex makes a lot of
             sense. There's something mystical about God making
             males and females.

ED: Go back to your story.

DONNIE: Right. All the way through high school and college I
             felt really conflicted. But, I had an out.

ED: What do you mean?

DONNIE: Toward the end of college, after I'd prayed and asked
             God to change me, I just gave up on Christianity. It just
             didn't work. And Christians even helped me to leave
             Christianity.

ED: There's a statement!

DONNIE: They did. By being so condemning. Not to me, because
             I never told any Christians I was gay. But just the way
             they talked about gays was so harsh and full of hate.
             Now *that's* exactly what Jesus meant by "judge not."
             They judged in the harshest way. And just like Jesus
             said, "Judge not, lest you be judged," so I judged them
             back. They condemned gays. I condemned them and
             left Christianity. For ten gay years.

ED: I don't blame you in the least.

DONNIE: But that didn't make me any more comfortable with
             being gay. Every relationship, every trip to the bars . . . I
             just knew it wasn't healthy.

ED: What about all those scientific discoveries proving
             people are born gay?

DONNIE: Proving?

ED: Yeah. I read in *Time* magazine, I think, about studies
             that were published in medical journals. They say
             there's some kind of genetic makeup to it.

DONNIE: Have you read these studies?

ED: No.

DONNIE: Well, I have—at least the ones they claim are so conclusive.

ED: And . . .

DONNIE: Did you ever take a basic science class where they talked about the scientific method?

ED: Back in college . . . freshman year, I think.

DONNIE: Me too. Those "conclusive" studies you read about are lousy science. They've all got an ax to grind, and they violate a lot of the rules of what constitutes a valid experiment. But nobody wants to blow the whistle on them or they'll be labeled "homophobic."

ED: You're saying that the studies are bogus?

DONNIE: Pretty close. They're certainly not conclusive. But people have accepted that there's a scientific basis for homosexuality.

ED: I don't know if I believe you. This sounds pretty suspect.

DONNIE: I don't blame you. But check it out for yourself. There aren't all that many studies, and the ones that *have* been published are pretty shaky. Besides, even if scientists did find some kind of genetic predisposition toward being gay, what would that prove?

ED: That people can't help it and we shouldn't condemn them for it.

DONNIE: You've been trained well, Ed.

ED: What's that supposed to mean?

DONNIE: Do you know what else has a genetic predisposition?

ED: No. What?

DONNIE: Alcoholism. Some people are genetically less able to handle alcohol. So should we say, "Eh. That's just how they're wired and they should just be drunks"?

ED: I think that's different.

DONNIE: In some ways, yes. But my point is that even if there is a

	genetic predisposition toward gayness, it doesn't mean it's a good thing.
ED:	Maybe. But let's go back to your saga. What was it that broke the cycle for you?
DONNIE:	That's a good way to put it. That last relationship . . . the one I said was pretty good . . . well, he broke up with me . . . because now *I* was the one who was verbally abusive. I remember looking at myself in the mirror after he moved out.
ED:	You lived together with someone?
DONNIE:	Oh, I'd lived with several guys. This last one seemed like it was going to last.
ED:	Sorry. I didn't mean to interrupt.
DONNIE:	It's okay. Anyway, when I looked in the mirror, it was like all sorts of things were hitting at the same time. He broke up with me. I realized I was the abusive jerk. I'd just had my thirtieth birthday. There was the Jesse Dirkhising story. And Oprah had a show about being gay!
ED:	Good old Oprah. I would guess that she'd make it seem fine to be gay, right?
DONNIE:	Now she sure would. But back then, she had a panel of ex-gays and ex-ex-gays.
ED:	Ex-ex-gays?
DONNIE:	The ex-gays were people who left the gay lifestyle behind. The ex-ex-gays were ones who tried that, saw that it didn't work, and went back to being gay.
ED:	Sounds more like a Geraldo show. Any cross-dressers?
DONNIE:	Stop.
ED:	Sorry.
DONNIE:	Here's what hit me. The ex-gays were calm. They were polite. They were pretty comfortable with their sexuality. The ex-ex-gays were just plain nasty. They were angry and abusive. They kept interrupting the people who were trying to say that being gay is not

	healthy. And I just had to admit, I needed to try this ex-gay thing.
ED:	So how'd you do that?
DONNIE:	This is another long story. Do you have time for dessert?
ED:	Yeah. I'll tell the waiter the next time I see him.
DONNIE:	Good. I'll give you the condensed version, though. I found a support group . . . one of those Exodus groups. Actually, Oprah showed a Web address on her show and I wrote it down. That connected me to something called, "Living Waters," a kind of program to help people come out of homosexuality. It was like thirty weeks long and incredibly intense. But it touched on all my issues—abuse as a child, low self-esteem, bad relationship with my father and other men in my family.
ED:	What kind of bad relationship with your father?
DONNIE:	It's amazing how prevalent a bad father-son relationship is among gays. But they dismiss it as if everyone's got a lousy father. Just read some of the stories of so-called gay role models. Newspapers run these stories a lot these days. Keep reading until you get to the fathers, how many gays grew up without them. I read this entire book arguing for gay marriage, how it's good for society and stuff like that. In the first chapter, the author talks about how his parents got divorced when he was twelve. You know how devastating it is for a boy to have his father leave at that crucial age?
ED:	I get the idea that *you* do.
DONNIE:	The sexual revolution of the sixties led to lots of divorces. It was only a matter of time before that led to a rise in homosexuality.
ED:	I don't see how.
DONNIE:	The free love of the sixties wasn't so free. It came with a price tag—maybe several. But one of them was a

dissatisfaction with just one sex partner for life. So men left their first wives and looked for more sexual fun. But it left a lot of young boys raised by mothers, and young girls feeling like they couldn't trust men. You couldn't ask for a better recipe to produce gay men and lesbians.

ED: Your parents got divorced?

DONNIE: It doesn't always work this way. My parents stayed together, but my father was distant. I just never connected with him. That's another cause of homosexuality.

ED: There's a gay guy at work who talks a bunch about how his father rejected him because he's gay.

DONNIE: Maybe it's the other way around.

ED: What do you mean?

DONNIE: Maybe it's not that his father rejected him because he's gay; maybe he became gay because his father rejected him.

ED: Or maybe you just want to rewrite his bio to fit your prejudices.

DONNIE: Maybe. But I've done a lot of research, and the stats are on my side—a bad father-son relationship figures prominently in a lot of gay people's stories.

ED: Hmm. So . . . you took this thirty-week class and came out straight?

DONNIE: I wish. Actually, I did wish. But it didn't work that way.

ED: Did you find some other program?

DONNIE: No. I wanted that program to be magic, and I told God that if I didn't turn straight within a year after graduating, I'd give up on him and Christianity and go back to being gay.

ED: And?

DONNIE: God's timetable is sometimes different than ours. Usually slower.

ED: So it didn't take, huh?

DONNIE: Not as much as I would've liked. The class was good,
            and it identified a lot of issues, but after a year with no
            desires for women, I plunged back into being gay. Lots
            of bars, lots of guys. Lots of disappointments.
ED: Have you been tested for AIDS?
DONNIE: Yes. I'm clean. Which, to be honest, is a miracle.
ED: I'll say. Keep going. I can't stand the suspense.
DONNIE: Well, when my second round of gayness left me at the
            same place as the first round, it really broke me. I was
            actually close to suicide.
ED: I can understand. It's like you can't be straight. But
            being gay is miserable.
DONNIE: Exactly. So guess where I decided to turn.
ED: I don't know.
DONNIE: Church.
ED: One of those gay churches, like you were talking about
            before?
DONNIE: No.
ED: Not the same kind of place where you felt rejected
            before!
DONNIE: Not the exact same church—but another Christian
            church.
ED: I'm hoping these people were nicer to you.
DONNIE: They were amazing. They were so accepting and
            real. I'd say they were the most important part of my
            healing.
ED: How so?
DONNIE: They had a great understanding of what grace is all
            about. Grace is a whole lot more than just being "nice."
ED: Define *grace* for me.
DONNIE: *Grace* is the realization that we're all sinners—far worse
            than we'd care to admit—but we're all redeemable.
ED: That doesn't help me much. When you defined *grace*
            you used another word I don't really understand—
            redeemable.

DONNIE:	Sorry. You're being a good newsman by pushing me with your questions.
ED:	I'm not trying to be difficult. I'm really trying to understand you.
DONNIE:	I know. *Redeemable* is a hard word to explain. Let me try it another way. Grace acknowledges our sin but doesn't think we're beyond forgiveness.
ED:	I get that. So we're all forgiven. That doesn't seem so amazing.
DONNIE:	If we're all just forgiven, no matter what, then I guess you're right. But that's not the Christian view of forgiveness. That kind of grace is cheap. So it doesn't really mean that much.
ED:	And your alternative is what?
DONNIE:	A costly grace. A grace that cost God a lot—it cost him his Son.
ED:	And this church talked about homosexuality a lot?
DONNIE:	Not that much. But they *did* talk about how we all need forgiveness, that we all have something that trips us up. And no one set of sins is easier to forgive than another. All of it is impossible to solve on our own. The only solution is Christ's death on the cross.
ED:	Sounds a bit heavy for me right now.
DONNIE:	Well . . . yeah, it is pretty intense. I'll just finish up with my story and cool it on the religious angle. If you ever want to talk about that, though, I'd be glad to.
ED:	Maybe.
DONNIE:	Fair enough. I'll just say that church helped me get all my wires straightened out.
ED:	Wires?
DONNIE:	That's how I usually talk about it. I needed to get my relationships with men healthy before getting them right with women. That was the problem I didn't take into account after the Living Waters program. I tried just dating women and nothing was happening.

ED: You had no desire for women? None?

DONNIE: Not really. I needed to go through a progression. First,
           I needed to relate to men in a healthy way. Nothing
           sexual. That took awhile, but these guys at this church
           helped me with that. They were able to love me
           and accept me and pray with me without anything
           sexual about it. Then came healthy relationships with
           women—just as friends. Then, much later, came the
           dating relationships with women—and desires. But it
           all took time.

ED: And now you're all fixed—no fantasies about men,
           good sex with your wife? . . . Wow. I can't believe I just
           said that. I'm sorry. That's so intrusive.

DONNIE: I don't mind. Really. I talk about these kinds of
           personal things all the time. I told you I was doing a
           radio interview . . . remember?

ED: Yeah.

DONNIE: I wasn't the one asking the questions. I was answering
           them. It was for a radio talk show about sex. I told my
           story, and people called in with questions about gays
           going straight.

ED: You're kidding. Just before we ran into each other?

DONNIE: Yeah.

ED: How'd it go?

DONNIE: Better than most.

ED: You do a lot of these?

DONNIE: A fair amount.

ED: I'd love to hear one of them sometime.

DONNIE: Actually, you're getting all the same stuff I say in those
           interviews right here. Anyway, I don't mind telling you
           about these things. Yes, I have sex with my wife, and
           yes, it's really good. There's almost something healing
           about sex with a woman that I never experienced with a
           man. It's hard to put into words. Let's just say that God
           knew what he was doing when he made us different.

ED: And looking at guys never turns you on?

DONNIE: Less and less. The healing process is gradual. But I'd be lying if I told you I never look at *some* guys without *some* attraction. The process of change isn't as instant as I'd like.

ED: God's timetable again.

DONNIE: Right. But the process is good—even if it's slower than I want it to be.

ED: You know, you seem pretty at ease talking about sex. It almost seems like in our society today, people either don't talk about it at all—like it's something dirty—or they talk about it too much, almost too casually—like it's nothing.

DONNIE: I call it the "Prude or Porn" phenomena.

ED: I'll bet those radio interviewers like that.

DONNIE: Either we feel ashamed about sex or we make it cheap and meaningless. It's really disturbing.

ED: You're right. I never hear a healthy alternative.

DONNIE: Prudishness doesn't treat sex the way it should be treated. And neither does porn. What we need are some people talking about sex as if it's profound and beautiful. It points us to another realm.

ED: What do you mean?

DONNIE: I need to warn you, I can't talk about sex for long without talking about God. Is that okay with you?

ED: Yeah. But I don't see how you make that connection.

DONNIE: I think sex is one of God's best gifts to people. There's nothing else that's both as pleasurable and as meaningful. Some things are pleasurable—although not as much as sex is. But those things aren't as profound.

ED: Like listening to music or looking at art or nature. Is that what you mean?

DONNIE: Yes. And other things are profound in meaning—like reading the Constitution or hearing some world

	leader make a speech at the U.N.—but they're not as pleasurable.
ED:	But I don't see how sex is so profound. It's just a physical thing.
DONNIE:	Ed, you don't really mean that, do you? Sex is just a physical thing? If it is, then I guess it really doesn't matter who you sleep with—male, female, whoever. If it's only a physical thing, why would your wife get ticked off if you came home and told her you slept with someone else today?
ED:	I never thought about it this way.
DONNIE:	When you deal with being gay and wanting to go straight and sexual addiction—things like that—you do a lot of thinking about sex. A lot!
ED:	I'll bet.
DONNIE:	So I really don't buy the line that sex is just a physical thing—and you don't either. No one does. They might say it but the way they treat sex shows otherwise. That's why I say I can't talk about sex without it pointing me to God.
ED:	I think part of why it's hard for me to think like you do—that sex is so important . . . how did you say it?
DONNIE:	Profound.
ED:	Yeah. It's because we're so messed up in our society today. There's so much sleeping around. In my office— you wouldn't believe it.
DONNIE:	I'm afraid I would.
ED:	It's like a soap opera. I don't want to cheat on my wife. Really. And I never have. But some people look at my wedding ring and think it means nothing.
DONNIE:	And so some people say, "Hey. Everybody's sleeping around. It's no big deal. What's the difference if it's a married person or a single person—or straights or gays?" But it sure leaves a lot of people hurt by the whole mess.

ED: You're not kidding. It's like there are no limits
           anymore. You can do anything and just claim it's your
           lifestyle choice and that makes it acceptable.

DONNIE: Did you know that there are pro-anorexia Web
           sites? They're for people who band together for
           support because they choose the lifestyle of starving
           themselves.

ED: That's sick!

DONNIE: There's a woman at my office who almost died from
           that, and now there are people who want to promote it
           and be proud of it.

ED: Man, you've really given me a lot to think about.

DONNIE: I didn't get to hear anything about you. I'm really
           sorry but I've got to get back to work. I feel bad that I
           monopolized things.

ED: Nah. Don't worry about it. I kept asking questions. Let's
           get together again. I can fill you in on what I'm up to.

DONNIE: That'd be great.

ED: But . . . do you have another few minutes?

DONNIE: Yeah. Why?

ED: This is difficult to talk about. I've got this nephew. I
           guess he's about sixteen now. He's just told his parents
           that he's gay. I think he's really messed up, though. He
           sounds so confused.

DONNIE: Mmm.

ED: He's my cousin's son—not technically my nephew . . . a
           second cousin, I guess. But we're pretty close.

DONNIE: It doesn't matter.

ED: Anyway, his mother—my cousin—she's really upset.
           She's pretty religious, but his father seems okay about
           it. They're divorced . . .

DONNIE: I was gonna ask, but I could have guessed.

ED: Yeah. It's like you were saying. I never connected those
           things.

DONNIE: So his father's okay about it.

ED: I'm not sure. His father's been out of the picture since
          the boy was like two.

DONNIE: That's so harmful for a young boy to lose his father at
          such a young age.

ED: Well, it's not like he died.

DONNIE: That actually would have been easier for the boy. I
          mean it.

ED: Really?

DONNIE: I could show you studies.

ED: Man! Anyway, his father says things to him like, "Hey.
          You're gay. It's okay. Let's move on."

DONNIE: But his mother's not okay about it.

ED: No. And she's the one who's got to deal with it. The
          father's in another state.

DONNIE: I've heard this story lots of times.

ED: So here's what I'm wondering. And I know this is
          awkward, but . . . would you be willing to talk to my
          nephew—I mean my cousin, sometime? About what
          you've gone through?

DONNIE: Would he be open to that?

ED: I don't know.

DONNIE: Why don't you talk to him?

ED: I would. But I don't have your experience. What would
          I say?

DONNIE: You could tell him about me. I think hearing it from
          you, a close relative—a close, male relative—would
          mean more than hearing it from me.

ED: That would be so weird.

DONNIE: Maybe you need to get past your fear of this issue.

ED: Maybe.

DONNIE: I'd be glad to talk to him, if he's up for it. But you need
          to talk to him first. If you want, I'll coach you through
          it. Here's my card with my e-mail address. Think about
          what you want to say, run it by me on e-mail, and I can
          give you some pointers.

ED: Thanks. This'll be hard.

DONNIE: Yeah. But it'll be good—for both of you. Check out
             Exodus's Web site before you talk to him. There's some
             good material there. Be careful that you don't promise
             a guarantee of change. My story isn't everyone's.

ED: Okay. Looks like I've got lots of homework to do.

DONNIE: I could send you a tape of one of my radio interviews.
             That might be a less threatening way to talk to him.
             You should listen to the tape first, though, and see if it
             would connect with him.

ED: That'd be great.

DONNIE: Do you have a card with your mailing address? I'll send
             you the tape and some written material.

ED: Here. Thanks. That would help me a lot.

DONNIE: Sure. I'd better go now.

ED: Me too. Hey, it was really great running into you.

DONNIE: Yeah. It sure was. Let's keep in touch.

ED: Absolutely.

DONNIE: And, Ed.

ED: Yeah?

DONNIE: When you talk to your nephew—cousin.

ED: Yeah?

DONNIE: Give him a hug.

❖

Keep the Conversation Going

- First Corinthians 6 would prove helpful as a rationale for
  what might otherwise seem unreasonable as well as out of
  step with our world today.
- Many very helpful books and online resources are now
  available about the Exodus movement. In particular, visit
  www.exodus-international.org and www.stonewallrevisited
  .com.

•   To name just a few helpful books, consider the following:

Bob Davies and Lela Gilbert, *Portraits of Freedom: 14 People
   Who Came Out of Homosexuality* (Downers Grove, Ill.:
   InterVarsity, 2001).
Mike Haley, *101 Frequently Asked Questions About
   Homosexuality* (Eugene, Ore.: Harvest House, 2004).
John and Anne Paulk, *Love Won Out* (Colorado Springs:
   Focus on the Family, 1999).

117   *Jesse Dirkhising died almost a year after Matthew
      Shepherd*: This is a true story. You can read more about
      it in many places by doing an Internet search. Note,
      especially, how gay writers agree with the version of
      the story presented in this dialogue.

122   *And yet there are some churches that say being gay isn't
      a sin. How do they interpret those verses?*: The best
      responses to so-called "gay theology" can be found in
      Joe Dallas, *A Strong Delusion* (Eugene, Ore.: Harvest
      House, 1996)—a relatively easy read; and Robert A. J.
      Gagnon, *The Bible and Homosexual Practice: Texts and
      Hermeneutics* (Nashville: Abringdon, 2002)—a very
      technical, scholarly work.

124   *Those "conclusive" studies you read about are lousy
      science*: For an up-to-date evaluation of scientific
      publications about homosexuality, see www.narth
      .com (NARTH stands for National Association for
      Research and Therapy of Homosexuality).

126   *I read this entire book arguing for gay marriage*:
      Jonathan Rausch, *Gay Marriage: Why It Is Good for
      Gays, Good for Straights, and Good for America* (New
      York: Henry Holt, 2004). The author mentions his
      parents' divorce on page 12.

127   *But I've done a lot of research and the stats are on my
      side*: See www.narth.com, especially papers on "Father
      Hunger and Homosexuality."

129   *The only solution is Christ's death on the cross*: An
      excellent explanation of grace can be found in John
      Stott, *Basic Christianity* (Grand Rapids: Eerdmans,
      1981).

134   *I could show you studies*: See www.narth.com.

Relaxing over Tea at Oat Fields

Skepticism Because of Hypocrisy, Hatred, and Evil in the Church

OAT FIELDS WHOLESOME GROCERS FINALLY reopened after months of re-modeling. Shoppers couldn't resist stopping by the café/lounge at the front of the store. The pamphlet describing the changes to the store encouraged shoppers to "explore the newest feature at Oat Fields and relax over a cup of herbal tea or sip a mug of our free-trade, shade-grown, organic coffee before or after shopping."

Barbara O'Malley and Kim Waters took the suggestion further than the pamphlet designer ever imagined. Why not meet every week before shopping for catching up, swapping coupons, and informing each other of any sales Oat Fields might be having? Staking out their claim to the corner table, the one with the softest cushioned chairs, they made a pact to meet every Monday at 9 a.m., after saying goodbye to their husbands, getting the kids off to school, and making their grocery lists. Their unofficial goal, over time, was to sample every one of the teas offered. Their self-imposed discipline was to finish tea and talk in time to hit the produce aisle by 9:30.

Barbara and Kim grew up within a few blocks of each other in Turnerville, graduated from high school together, went to different colleges, but wound up back in Turnerville after their collegiate days. They married Turnerville guys within a year of each other, bought houses less then two miles apart, and had three children almost on identical schedules. Now, in their mid-forties, with three teenagers each, they connect more out of habit than anything else. On the surface, they look so similar. Deeper than that, however, the similarities are minimal.

October 4: Tazo Awake Black Tea

BARBARA: Wow! This is strong. I like it. I hope this stuff lives up to its name. I could use the caffeine today.

KIM: Too strong for me.

BARBARA: How was your weekend?

KIM: Okay. Nothing special. Todd was glued to the television. How many football games can you watch in a weekend?

BARBARA: It *is* amazing, isn't it?

KIM: I don't suppose they made some big announcement at your church yesterday about that stupid priest—the one down in Georgia who admitted to all those sexual abuses. They don't usually brag about such things, huh?

BARBARA: No, they didn't. And brag isn't—

KIM: Can you believe that? All those boys over all those years!

BARBARA: Well—

KIM: It's one thing for politicians to mess around. But priests? They're all such a bunch of hypocrites.

BARBARA: All of them?

KIM: How many of our presidents were fooling around? Everyone knows FDR was. And JFK had his thing with Marilyn Monroe. And of course we now know more about Clinton's sex life than we ever wanted to. Why don't we just admit that politicians all do it and we should just get over it. I mean, maybe they need to—like it's part of the whole power-trip thing.

BARBARA: You think it's okay they sleep around?

KIM: I don't see what harm it does to our economy or the rest of our country's interests. It doesn't threaten national security if they mess around.

BARBARA: Are you sure of that?

KIM: What about Nixon? Do you think he had affairs?

BARBARA: If Todd was having sex with someone from his office, you wouldn't mind?

KIM: Are you kidding? I'd nail his you-know-what to the wall.

BARBARA: Well, then—

KIM: But priests?! That's just disgusting. And I think it's nothing new. I think this kind of thing has been happening for years—maybe the whole history of the church. And we're just finding out about it now because people are finally being honest.

BARBARA: But—

KIM: And I think it's great that people are being honest about this. It's better than all those conservative hypocrites who talk about moral values all the time and then turn around and cheat on their wives. All you Christians are always raving about Rush Limbaugh. How many times has he been divorced now? Three?

BARBARA: I don't like Rush Limbaugh, and I know a lot of Christians who think he doesn't represent them. He's conservative but that doesn't mean he's Christian.

KIM: And I don't even need to *start* about all those televangelists who are having affairs.

BARBARA: All of them?

KIM: And all these people who are now saying they were abused as altar boys by priests. It's horrible, isn't it? How are these people ever going to get their lives back? I think the church should pay them a million dollars each—or maybe more!

BARBARA: The caffeine in this tea sure has worked for you, girl.

KIM: Doesn't it bother you that there are so many hypocrites in the church?

BARBARA: It sounds like what's bothering you is a lot worse than hypocrisy. Don't you think?

KIM: Like what?

BARBARA: Priests abusing altar boys! That's downright evil, not just hypocritical.

KIM: You're right.

BARBARA: So what really bothers you is sin—not hypocrisy.

KIM: It's not that easy, Barbara. I know that everybody sins. I sure do. But this is something different.

BARBARA: How so?

KIM: It's saying one thing and doing another. Isn't that the definition of hypocrisy?

BARBARA: Sounds right.

KIM: So, these priests say, or at least they believe, that you shouldn't have sex with boys but then that's what they're doing. That's hypocrisy, pure and simple.

BARBARA: But what bothers you isn't their hypocrisy as much as their sin. They sinned against those boys.

KIM: I think it's that they're two-faced low-lifes, that's what I think.

BARBARA: And if they said they think it's okay to have sex with boys, and then they did it, it wouldn't bother you? Because then they wouldn't be hypocrites.

KIM: That's sick.

BARBARA: It sounds like you're saying the worst thing about them is that they're two-faced. But aren't there some things worse than hypocrisy?

KIM: Uh . . .

BARBARA: Maybe some of this honesty you're so crazy about isn't all that good.

KIM: Sometimes I think Christians are their own worst enemies. You guys want to change the world and inflict your values on everyone, and just look at how you live.

BARBARA: Are you referring to me when you say, "you"?

KIM: You know what I mean.

BARBARA: No, I don't. Are you calling me a hypocrite?

KIM: Oh don't be silly. You're great. But all the other Christians I know are different than you.

BARBARA: All? Really? Do you really mean all?

KIM: No. But it sure seems like most of them.

BARBARA: You know what? I think you're being unfair.

KIM: You don't know the people I know.

BARBARA: Sure I do. I know just about all the people you know! We grew up together. And I think you're being too harsh.

KIM: It still bothers me that you Christians don't practice what you preach.

BARBARA: Why do you think that is?

KIM: Beats me!

BARBARA: I think I have some ideas. Want to hear them?

KIM: Yes. But not now. I've gotta get started early today.

BARBARA: Next week?

KIM: Sure.

BARBARA: We're going herbal next week. This much caffeine in your veins is a little scary.

KIM: Ha!

October 11: Celestial Seasonings Berry Zinger

BARBARA: I like this tea! I think I taste a difference when it's loose in the teapot instead of in tea bags.

KIM: It's too flowery. Fruity, I mean. I'm not so crazy about it.

BARBARA: It'll keep you calm, though.

KIM: Oh, you know me. I'm naturally caffeinated.

BARBARA: That's a good way to put it.

KIM: Yesterday I finally got to read the whole Sunday paper.

I never get the time to do that. It's always rush, rush, rush in our house. Even on Sunday. Somebody always needs something washed or sewn and it's always me who has to do the work. I don't even get a break on Sundays. Isn't that supposed to be a day of rest? Not for mothers, that's for sure.

BARBARA: Anything good in the paper?

KIM: I saw something about what we were talking about last week. There was this article about the whole history of the church being filled with horrible things.

BARBARA: Filled? Is that the word they used?

KIM: First you had the Crusades. Then there's all this racism among Christians. Look at all those southern churches that are still segregated today.

BARBARA: Still? Really?

KIM: And there was this whole section about anti-Semitism in the church—like all those passion plays that made the Jews out to be the bad guys. Did you know that Shakespeare was anti-Semitic? That Shylock character—

BARBARA: Wait a minute. You're mixing a lot of things together. I don't know about Shakespeare, but even if he *was* anti-Semitic, that's different than the church being anti-Semitic.

KIM: I know. I was just saying.

BARBARA: You're right, though. Some Christians have been racist or anti-Semitic.

KIM: The Ku Klux Klan burns crosses, don't they? What's that all about? And didn't the Nazis claim to be Christian?

BARBARA: Did that article say that?

KIM: No. I just heard that somewhere.

BARBARA: Please—listen to yourself. You're lumping Will and me together with Shakespeare, the Nazis, and the KKK. That's not fair.

KIM: Well, you will admit that the church has had its bad
              moments.
BARBARA: No question. And it's bad enough as it is. Just don't
              make it seem worse than it really is.
KIM: This article said that religion has been the source for
              all the problems in the world.
BARBARA: Do you believe that?
KIM: Well what about the Crusades? Weren't they what the
              church was all about back then?
BARBARA: No. That was *some* of the church. And all these things
              you've been talking about only apply to *some* in the
              church. Don't make it such a universal thing.
KIM: I thought the church's leadership was behind the
              Crusades. And what about the Salem witch trials?
BARBARA: Kim, take a breath, would you! You can't just lump all
              these things together.
KIM: I'm just saying—
BARBARA: You're just saying what? That every single Christian in
              the history of the church has been a jerk?
KIM: No.
BARBARA: What then?
KIM: This guy who wrote the article. He quoted some other
              writer. I forget who. He said he wished everybody
              could just be apathetic about religion. He said the
              world would be a whole lot better off. He had this
              made-up word to describe his religion. He called it
              "apatheism." He was apathetic about whether God
              existed. So he wasn't an atheist. He just didn't care.
              And he didn't care about other people's beliefs either.
              So he'd never tell anyone their religion was bad or
              wrong or anything.
BARBARA: And he said that's how everyone should be.
KIM: Yeah.
BARBARA: Is that what you want to be?
KIM: I'm just telling you what he wrote.

BARBARA: But what do you think about it? Do you want to join
             the religion of apatheism?

KIM: Maybe. I do think religion's been the source of a lot
             of pain. Those guys who crashed the planes into the
             towers in New York were religious fanatics, you know.

BARBARA: You must really like John Lennon's song, "Imagine."

KIM: You know Albert, the guy who cuts my hair?

BARBARA: You've told me about him before.

KIM: You know, he hears a lot of people talk about religion
             and politics. He says the people you've really got to
             watch out for are the ones most committed to their
             religion. The fanatics. They're the worst.

BARBARA: And it would be better if we were all . . . what did you
             call it? Apatheistic?

KIM: Yeah. You don't think so, do you?

BARBARA: It just sounds to me like apatheism is pretty extreme
             too.

KIM: Extreme?

BARBARA: I take it back. It sounds mean!

KIM: No it's not.

BARBARA: I think it is.

KIM: You're wrong, Barbara.

BARBARA: You're not sounding too apathetic about my beliefs
             right now. Wouldn't it be bad to be apathetic about
             people who were dying of starvation or disease?

KIM: You can't tell me that religion's always been such a
             great thing. And you can't tell me that there haven't
             been a whole ton of hypocrites in the church.

BARBARA: It doesn't sound to me like I can tell you anything.
             But let me try. I don't deny there's been a lot of
             terrible things done in the name of religion.

KIM: That's all I'm saying.

BARBARA: Ahhh, but I don't think it's *all* you're saying. I think
             you're saying much more than that. And that's where
             I think you're going too far.

KIM: I've just seen a lot of it. Okay?

BARBARA: Like what?

KIM: I don't want to talk about it.

BARBARA: All right. Just be careful that you don't make a
            minority of people represent the whole church. That
            wouldn't be fair.

KIM: I'll try.

BARBARA: And you might want to rethink this apathetic thing.
            Some of the worst evil this world has ever known
            hasn't come from religious fanatics—but from a
            different kind of fanatic. Hitler wasn't religious. Stalin
            was definitely atheist. The Communists in China
            killed people by the thousands, just for disagreeing
            with their regime.

KIM: But what about the Crusades?

BARBARA: You really like that one, don't you? I don't know what
            to say about the Crusades, Kim. I don't know much
            about them. They were bad, okay? But the church
            has done a lot of good things. And they didn't feed
            hungry people and things like that by being apathetic.
            And the good things really fit with what Christianity
            is all about. The Crusades don't fit.

KIM: Albert says you just have to take things in
            moderation.

BARBARA: That doesn't sound very moderate to me.

KIM: Huh?

BARBARA: You'd never feed starving people in Africa by taking
            everything in moderation. Going halfway around
            the world, raising all that money to do that, takes a
            certain kind of extremism—a good kind. So I don't
            think moderation is all it's cracked up to be. Sorry.
            Don't tell Albert.

KIM: Maybe I should show you this article.

BARBARA: Maybe. I'll read it, if you want me to. I'll show it to
            Will, too. He really likes talking about this.

KIM: I wish Todd did. He's only interested in football.

BARBARA: If you want to talk about the article some more next
            week, that would be fine with me. Right now, I better
            get started shopping. I've got a long list this week.

KIM: Me too.

October 18: Whittard Original

BARBARA: Ooh. I like this tea. This might be the best one we've
            had so far.

KIM: I steeped mine too long. It's bitter.

BARBARA: Here. Take a sip of mine and see what you think.

KIM: No. That's okay. I'll be all right.

BARBARA: How was your weekend?

KIM: It was fine until my mother called last night.

BARBARA: What's wrong?

KIM: Nothing, really. It's just that—she's my mother. Even
            when there's nothing wrong, it's a drain talking to
            her. Every time I get off the phone with her, I feel like
            I could use a drink.

BARBARA: I'm sorry to hear that.

KIM: They want to come visit.

BARBARA: Is that good news or bad news?

KIM: She finds a new way to insult me every time she
            visits. It's uncanny. Usually it's some kind of moral
            putdown. You're not good enough, or you're not
            raising the girls to be ladies, or why don't you take
            them to church more, or you're not letting them date
            boys, are you?

BARBARA: When does she want to come?

KIM: Oh, that would be far too precise for my mother.
            Schedule an actual date for something to happen?
            Are you kidding? No, we have to just talk about it
            for months. That almost makes it worse—like an
            impending storm or something.

BARBARA: Would it help if I changed the subject?

KIM: Oh yes.

BARBARA: Okay. I did read that article you dropped by—the one on all the hypocrites in the church.

KIM: What did you think?

BARBARA: I think it made a lot of sense . . . and I've decided to quit being a Christian. I'm now an atheist.

KIM: What?

BARBARA: Well, there aren't any atheist hypocrites, are there?

KIM: Are you for real?

BARBARA: No, I'm just kidding. I thought you'd like that.

KIM: I'm not laughing.

BARBARA: Sorry. I'll be serious. I actually *did* think he made some good points, but I think he put a whole lot of things together, all under the title of hypocrisy. I'm not sure that's a good way to think about it.

KIM: I never realized how messed up the church really is. I knew there were problems, and I've always been suspicious of all the money they're always asking for. But, man, he pointed out a lot of bad stuff. Did you know all this?

BARBARA: Some of it. Like I was saying, though, I don't think it's helpful to call it all hypocrisy. Some of it is evil. Some of it is people simply failing to live up to what they hold to be good. But that's different than being a hypocrite.

KIM: But some of it *is* hypocrisy, right?

BARBARA: Of course. But maybe I need to know what you mean when you say *hypocrisy*. What do you think that word means?

KIM: I don't know. Didn't we talk about this before? How about . . . saying one thing and doing another?

BARBARA: I think that depends on why you're doing the other thing.

KIM: Huh?

BARBARA:	Let's say one of your daughter's high school teachers is always lecturing about not doing drugs. Then it turns out he's getting drunk at home.
KIM:	Perfect example. Pure hypocrisy.
BARBARA:	Is it? Let's say he's an alcoholic who really wants to stop drinking but he just can't—unless he finds some AA group to help him.
KIM:	You're making excuses for this guy?
BARBARA:	No. I'm saying that's different than if this same teacher is telling the kids not to do drugs, but then outside of school he gets drunk, smokes dope, and says that's perfectly fine.
KIM:	I'm confused. Are you saying that's worse than the alcoholic?
BARBARA:	They're both bad. I don't know which one is worse. It doesn't matter. What *does* matter is that the alcoholic isn't a hypocrite. He's just a failure. Do you see the difference?
KIM:	I've always wondered if that guy who's the head of the P.E. department is an alcoholic. What's his name?
BARBARA:	I don't know.
KIM:	He just looks like someone who'd get drunk a lot.
BARBARA:	I don't know who you mean. But . . . did you get my point? If someone says one thing but then fails to practice what they preach, it could mean that they're just weak—not a hypocrite. But if they say one thing, "Doing drugs is bad," but they really don't mean it—they really think doing drugs is fine—that's a hypocrite.
KIM:	I'd want both of them to get fired. I think it's crazy that these teachers get tenure—so they can never get fired. What other job on the planet has that kind of thing?
BARBARA:	That's another topic. Let's save that for another day.
KIM:	Do you know who I mean? The P.E. guy? What's his name?

BARBARA: I really don't know. I'm sorry. Let's go back to the article. When he talked about the priests who are abusing those children—I already said this last week, I think—but the abuse isn't really a case of hypocrisy because the priests weren't saying that what they did was okay. They admitted that it was sick. Their sin was far worse than hypocrisy. They weren't having some kind of pedophile-pride parade.

KIM: Oh, that's so disgusting.

BARBARA: I know. And I think they know it, too.

KIM: If they don't get fired, I'm losing any faith I ever had in the church.

BARBARA: Didn't the word for hypocrite come from ancient Greek drama? The actors put a mask in front of their faces. It was like they were pretending to be one thing but they were really something else.

KIM: What about in the article where it talked about all the racism in the church—like segregated churches down south. You remember that?

BARBARA: I do. And I wish I could prove him wrong—but I think he's probably right. That kind of thing happens a lot.

KIM: So which is that? Hypocrisy or evil?

BARBARA: You know, when you ask it like that, it almost seems like it doesn't matter anymore. It's really disturbing, isn't it? It's very upsetting.

KIM: Jesus really hated hypocrites, didn't he?

BARBARA: Yes. He came down really hard on religious hypocrites, and I think I know why. Those people are supposed to be representing God. And what the people in the article did is like the *worst* kind of false advertising, and God doesn't want people to think he's racist, or evil, or that he thinks it's okay to abuse young boys.

KIM: Hmm.

BARBARA: Does that make sense?

KIM: I think so. I think you're on to something. Maybe
              you should write a letter to the paper—you know—
              following up on that article.

BARBARA: Maybe. But I didn't like the writer's whole tone in that
              article. He was really sarcastic. I'm not defending the
              people he was writing about. But he just sounded so
              self-righteous. Ironic, isn't it? He's saying how self-
              righteous all these religious people are and how bad
              that is, but he sounded worse than any of them.

KIM: I didn't think of that. But now that you say it—yeah.
              He was pretty arrogant.

BARBARA: Sometimes—and I'm not saying this is always the
              case—but sometimes people focus on this thing
              about hypocrites in the church as a way to justify
              their own sin. I don't know if that's the thing with
              this writer but I'm just saying it's a possibility.

KIM: I've read other things by him and he's always
              sarcastic.

BARBARA: Well, it would take someone who knows him better
              to figure all that out. So I'll stop and not say anything
              more about him.

KIM: Guess I'd better start shopping.

BARBARA: You didn't drink your tea.

KIM: I told you, I steeped it too long. Next week I'm setting
              a timer.

BARBARA: You know, I have a few more thoughts on this topic.
              Would it be okay if we talk about it some more?

KIM: Sure.

October 25: Stash Premium Green Tea

BARBARA: I thought we'd try some green tea today. What do you
              think?

KIM: It's okay. I've never really liked green tea. I know it's

good for you and all that but, I don't know. It's just all
right.

BARBARA: Are you okay?

KIM: Not really. This is a hard time of year for me.

BARBARA: It *is* kind of gray and cloudy a lot.

KIM: It's not the weather. Do you mind if we just start
            shopping now? We can try for tea again next week.

BARBARA: Sure. Are you sure you don't want to talk about what's
            going on?

KIM: Oh, I don't know. It's just that . . . Oh, you wouldn't
            understand.

BARBARA: Kim, what's bothering you?

KIM: Just leave me alone, would you? Just leave me alone!

Kim gets up from the table and storms away—madder than
Barbara can ever remember seeing her. At first Barbara simply sits,
stunned, but then she gets up to follow her. Kim throws some fruit
and vegetables in plastic bags, almost without thinking, and turns
the corner to an aisle lined with magazines and cosmetics. Barbara
catches up to her.

BARBARA: Kim, I promise I'll leave you alone if that's what you
            really want. But are you sure you don't want to talk?
            I get the idea you need to sort some things out. Did
            Todd and you have a fight?

KIM: If you ever tell Todd about this, I'll never talk to you
            again.

BARBARA: Oh.

KIM: Look. Todd doesn't know about what I go through
            every year around this time. He's not blind, and
            he knows something's happening, but I just keep

changing the subject every time he asks why I'm such a creep at the end of October.

BARBARA: Is this some kind of Halloween thing?

KIM: Ha! That's funny. I never thought of that. Maybe that's what I should tell him—that I'm a witch, not a . . . No, it's nothing like that.

BARBARA: Did somebody die around this time?

KIM: *[choking back tears]* Yes.

BARBARA: Who?

KIM: My baby.

BARBARA: What? When was this?

KIM: *[taking a deep breath, looking around to see if anyone else is in the aisle]* In my junior year of college. You remember I broke up with Billy the summer before our junior year?

BARBARA: Of course.

KIM: Well, I went back to college mad as a hornet. I was just so ticked off that he dumped me and I decided I was going to find some other guy as fast as I could. And I was dead set on finding someone the exact opposite of Billy. I wanted some fraternity guy. So I went to every frat party I could find in the first week back to school.

BARBARA: This was like almost twenty years ago, right?

KIM: Nineteen. But who's counting.

BARBARA: Wow.

KIM: It was lots of fun—for a while. Lots of beer, that's for sure. I just was tired of being the good girl—you know, get my degree, find a husband, graduate, have babies. I wanted to see what it was like to be the wild one for a change.

BARBARA: How long did that last?

KIM: Not that long. By mid-October I was pregnant, and my frat boy wanted nothing to do with me.

BARBARA: Oh my.

KIM: Barbara, I know you're against abortion. You even
                went to one of those marches, didn't you?

BARBARA: A couple.

KIM: Well, I'm against abortion too, but it's not that simple.
                People throw around the word *choice* all the time, but
                there was no choice for me. I was alone and confused
                and who knows how screwed up my hormones were at
                that time. I couldn't have even made a decent decision
                about what to eat in the cafeteria. I was angry. I was
                scared. I just panicked and went to the clinic across
                the street from the campus. It was October 29, eleven
                thirty in the morning. And every year since then, I
                have the hardest time making it through the end of
                October. I can't tell you how great it is to turn the
                calendar to November.

BARBARA: I'm so sorry.

KIM: And there weren't a lot of people to turn to back
                then. Seemed like two options—some nice people to
                hold your hand while you're lying on a cold table and
                doing what you said you'd never do, or some fanatical
                Christians who were blowing up abortion clinics.

BARBARA: Oh my.

KIM: So that's why I'm not too keen on going with you and
                Will to your church every time you invite Todd and
                me. I'm glad your girls keep inviting our kids. I guess.
                I don't know. I guess I want them to find some kind of
                religion. And you and Will are different, but all I ever
                got from religion was condemnation for being a baby
                killer.

BARBARA: Do you want to go sit down?

KIM: No. I just need to forget about it. One more week and
                it'll be November.

BARBARA: Does it get any easier to deal with as the years go by?

KIM: Are you kidding? I think it's getting harder. Beats the
                heck out of me why that is.

BARBARA:	And you've never told Todd?
KIM:	No. He doesn't need to know about my past. I don't want to know who he slept with before we met and he doesn't need to hear about my junior year September sex-a-thon. It was a long time ago.
BARBARA:	Kim, when we went to those pro-life rallies . . . You're right, there are some pretty mean-spirited people in those crowds, but most of them were . . . well, like me. If you think I'm different than a lot of Christians, you should meet some of these people. There are a lot of us who don't blow up clinics or call people murderers.
KIM:	Hmm.
BARBARA:	Some of the women in those crowds have had abortions themselves. And the reason they're marching is because they don't think other women should go through what they did.
KIM:	That's for sure.
BARBARA:	Our church . . . I know you don't like it when I talk about church, but please hear me out. Our church supports this center that helps women with unplanned pregnancies. I'm sorry there wasn't one near you nineteen years ago.
KIM:	Why are you telling me this? It's a little late, don't you think?
BARBARA:	No, not really. They have a few support groups for women who've had abortions. They call them post-abortion stress groups. You might want to think about calling them.
KIM:	Now? Nineteen years later? Sure, and what do I tell Todd? That I'm at some sewing-club meeting? Please.
BARBARA:	Some women in the group had their abortions a long time ago. You might not be the oldest one there. I think they have groups for women our age. You wouldn't be in some group with a bunch of college

KIM:	girls. In fact, I think the average age for women in one of the groups is around thirty-five.
KIM:	And what do I tell my daughters?
BARBARA:	I don't know, but I'll bet other people there have had to deal with questions like that. If you want, I'd even go with you.
KIM:	Listen, I really need to shop. Todd's having some people from his office over for dinner tomorrow night. I've got to make a fancy meal. It'll help take my mind off things. And then I'll get through the week and I'll be fine.
BARBARA:	Are you sure?
KIM:	No, I'm not sure. But, it's worked every other year. So I'll just hope for the best.
BARBARA:	If you want to talk some more—
KIM:	Right. I'll call you. Look, I've really got to go. Let's just drop it, okay?
BARBARA:	Okay. Do you still want to meet next Monday for tea?
KIM:	Yes. And I'll drink the tea, I promise.
BARBARA:	Good.
KIM:	Barbara . . . Look . . . I'm sorry if I was rude to you. It's just . . .
BARBARA:	It's okay.
KIM:	Next week will be better.
BARBARA:	Good. Um . . . I don't know how this will come across but . . . I'll be praying for you this week.
KIM:	Thanks. That comes across . . . great. Really.
BARBARA:	See you next week.

November 1: Twinings Earl Gray

KIM:	Barbara, I'm really sorry about last week. I was rude to you. I was just upset. You know—
BARBARA:	Don't worry about it. I'm glad you told me what you're going through. How are you doing?

KIM:	Fine. It's November!
BARBARA:	I know but . . . I mean . . . Are you going to be okay. . . in the long run, I mean?
KIM:	I don't know. I hope so. But this year did seem harder than other years. I don't understand it. I keep thinking, as time goes on, this whole memory should fade. And I thought it was—but this year. Whew! I don't get it.
BARBARA:	I'm not surprised that the whole memory of it won't just disappear.
KIM:	Maybe it's because our girls are beginning to talk about dating. Susan's going to the homecoming dance! She's all excited and talking about getting a dress. Have you seen the kinds of things these girls wear? Todd's talking about buying a gun rack for our living room to show all these boys who want to date our daughters.
BARBARA:	Ha! I don't blame him.
KIM:	So maybe I'm just worried that she'll make the same mistakes I did. Do you think that could have brought it to the surface?
BARBARA:	Maybe. Doesn't sound out of the question.
KIM:	Yesterday was really hard for me. All three of the girls went to church with friends of theirs. Todd and I stayed home. That was nice actually—to have some time alone. But when the girls got back, they all asked why we don't go to church as a family.
BARBARA:	What'd you say?
KIM:	Well, you know. They just don't accept our answers anymore like they used to when they were younger. They're teenagers now. They argue with everything we say. They're all going to be lawyers, I swear.
BARBARA:	What answers?
KIM:	Oh, you know . . . "We just don't go to church. That's all. We're not religious." When we used to say that,

it was fine. It was like telling them we're Norwegian
so we don't go to the German club or something. But
now, they're like, "Why not? Why aren't we religious?
What happened? What's wrong with us?" They were
like an interrogation squad.

BARBARA: So what did you tell them?

KIM: I was like, "We just don't, okay?" But Todd starts talking
to them real respectful like and being really sensitive.
Maybe it's because he got to sleep in. He was so nice.

BARBARA: Great.

KIM: No, it's not great. I mean . . . yes, it's great that he
was so sensitive and all . . . but not about religion, for
crying out loud. This is not the topic to start being
compassionate about.

BARBARA: You're kidding, right?

KIM: Of course, I am. It was really great to see him
interacting with the girls that way. And now he's
talking about us going to church as a family! You
know, with Christmas coming up and all.

BARBARA: Wow.

KIM: But I'm not feeling too good about this. I wasn't
objecting—on the outside that is. I didn't say
anything. But on the inside I'm not feeling good about
this at all.

BARBARA: Why do you suppose that is?

KIM: Barbara, I've just had some bad experiences with
church people. I just think there are a lot of phonies
in churches. I'm sorry. I don't mean you.

BARBARA: Actually, I agree with you.

KIM: You do?

BARBARA: Yeah. There are a lot of jerks in the church.

KIM: So why do you still go? Why do you still want to be a
part of that?

BARBARA: Hmm. Well, first of all, not everyone who goes to a
church is a Christian. You know that, right?

KIM: Sure.

BARBARA: That's one of the unique things about Christianity.
            It's not something you can be born into. Just because
            your parents are Christians doesn't mean you're one.
            In fact, that almost makes the problem worse.

KIM: I don't understand.

BARBARA: Let's just say there are a lot of people who think
            they're Christians—just because their parents are
            or just because they joined a church. But that's not
            how you become a Christian. It involves an inner
            change—like a second birth. If you haven't had that
            rebirth and you're going to church, thinking you're a
            Christian, you might be doing more harm than good.

KIM: False advertising.

BARBARA: Right. And I'm afraid there's a lot of that in our
            country today.

KIM: But why aren't there more Christians like you and
            Will?

BARBARA: You're far too kind, Kim. We've got plenty of our own
            junk. If you just hang around us more, you wouldn't
            think we're such saints.

KIM: Oh, c'mon now.

BARBARA: To tell you the truth, I think my problems are a lot
            worse than hypocrisy.

KIM: Get out of here!

BARBARA: I'm serious. You don't hear the kinds of things
            going on inside my head, or the way I talk to Will
            sometimes. But don't you see . . . that's exactly
            why I'm a Christian . . . because I'm such a sinner.
            Christianity's the best place for hypocrites and
            sinners because it's the one place we can get past our
            junk and move on.

KIM: So why don't more Christians move on? There are a
            whole lot of Christians who don't seem to get their act
            together.

BARBARA: Well, first of all, you're right. We should be getting
            better. If we're really growing as Christians, we
            should be changing, and I'm not sure why that's not
            happening. But on the other hand—how did you say
            it, "getting our act together"? That's exactly the wrong
            way to think about it.

KIM: Why?

BARBARA: We *can't* get our act together. If we could, we wouldn't
            need Jesus. Becoming a Christian happens to
            someone when they realize that they can't get their
            act together—unless God does the changing. But even
            then, being a Christian doesn't mean you're perfect.

KIM: Oh. I see what you mean.

BARBARA: You know what I think? I think the church might
            actually have a higher percentage of jerks or
            hypocrites or messed up people than the rest of
            society.

KIM: Why would that be?

BARBARA: Lots of reasons. I'm not sure which one is the main
            reason, but first of all, nice people—people who kind
            of have it together—don't turn to God that much.
            They don't think they need him. But needy people do.
            So the average church has a lot of needy people and
            fewer so-called together people. Remember, it was
            always the outcasts that came to Jesus when he was
            on earth. He said, "It's not the healthy who need a
            doctor, but the sick."

KIM: So some people don't need Jesus?

BARBARA: No. That's not what he meant. We're all sick—
            spiritually, that is. But no one goes to the doctor
            unless he admits he's sick. As long as you think you've
            got it together, you don't look to God to save you or
            help you or heal you.

KIM: Well, let me tell you something. If you're right, people
            have to get to the point where they're willing to admit

on their own they need God. They can't be forced into it. That's what I think people have always tried to do to me—make me feel like I'm the worst sinner on the planet. Especially after that whole junior year thing I told you about.

BARBARA: You're right. I'm so sorry people treated you like that.

KIM: I don't know that what I did was wrong? I'm not stupid.

BARBARA: It still hurts, doesn't it? I mean, the way people treated you.

KIM: Uh-huh.

BARBARA: Look, I'm not trying to make excuses for anybody, but why do you think this kind of behavior bothers you so much?

KIM: What behavior?

BARBARA: People treating you so badly . . . being mean . . . all this stuff about hypocrisy.

KIM: You're saying it shouldn't bother me?

BARBARA: No. No. No. Just the opposite. I'm saying it *should* bother you, and that it's a sign that there *is* a God who's good and loving. The very fact that jerks bother you is proof that there's something better out there.

KIM: I'm not sure what I think about all that.

BARBARA: That's okay. Would you like to hear another reason that there are some judgmental people in the church? Maybe they've got high expectations about the way things should be. And when they get disappointed, they have more of a reaction. It's like there's this internal tension—things are supposed to be better but they're not.

KIM: That's no excuse.

BARBARA: No, it isn't. I told you, I'm not trying to make excuses. But it does help to understand. An explanation isn't an excuse.

KIM: A lot of Christians have told me that I'm just not

sincere about wanting to believe in God . . . that if I was just sincere enough, God would zap me and I'd have all the answers I'm looking for.

BARBARA: Then you do want to believe in God? Or maybe it's more than believe in him . . . you want to follow him?

KIM: I think so. I don't know. I don't see why he'd want me as one of his followers.

BARBARA: Wait a minute. What are you saying?

KIM: I don't know. Look, we're late. It's after nine thirty.

BARBARA: We can flex this one time. Can't we?

KIM: We could. But . . . I'd rather not . . . I'm not mad like I was last week. I just need time to digest this, okay?

BARBARA: Sure.

KIM: Besides, I think we're going to church this Sunday. Yikes! I think I'm going to have lots of questions for you over our little cup of tea next week. We might have to get a whole pot of tea.

BARBARA: I'd like that.

KIM: Yeah? We'll just see if you like it or not.

November 8: Republic of Tea Oolong

BARBARA: They say that Oolong tea is halfway between black and green tea. I think this is what they serve at some Chinese restaurants. What do you think?

KIM: Yeah. Not as strong as black but not as . . . I don't know . . . weak as green. I think this is my kind of tea.

BARBARA: I like this teapot idea. This is what we should do every week.

KIM: Yeah.

BARBARA: You seem kind of down. Anything wrong?

KIM: You're going to hate me, Barbara.

BARBARA: What do you mean? Why would I hate you?

KIM: I chickened out on going to church yesterday.

BARBARA:	Oh.
KIM:	Todd and the girls went. I said I didn't feel good and I slept in.
BARBARA:	Hey, if you didn't feel all right—
KIM:	I was fine. Well, I didn't feel all that great, but if I really wanted to go, I would've gone. It was just an excuse. I feel terrible. It was like I lied to them.
BARBARA:	Well, how'd they like it?
KIM:	They loved it!
BARBARA:	Including Todd?
KIM:	I think he liked it the most! It's like I've got a house full of religious fanatics now.
BARBARA:	No, you don't!
KIM:	Okay, so I'm exaggerating. They did like it, though, and they really want me to come next Sunday.
BARBARA:	This is something. What a story!
KIM:	The girls had a lot of fun. This youth group thing was all they talked about over lunch.
BARBARA:	So . . . what do you think?
KIM:	I'd rather have them there than out drinking with the kids you see on Friday nights after the football games.
BARBARA:	No, I mean for you. Do you think you'll join them?
KIM:	I kinda have to, don't you think?
BARBARA:	Are you asking me if I think you should go to church? I'm not exactly unbiased.
KIM:	I know. It's just that I've had this thing against church for so long—I've been saying that I just can't stand all those phonies and now . . . well . . . I don't know.
BARBARA:	Let's talk about this a little. You don't think that all Christians are phonies, do you?
KIM:	Definitely not.
BARBARA:	People love the cliché, "the church is full of hypocrites." But you don't think it's *full* of them, do you? Maybe just a percentage?
KIM:	Right.

BARBARA: And you don't think that Christianity teaches
            people that they should be jerks or hateful or mean,
            right?

KIM: No. Not at all. Todd said the pastor's sermon
            yesterday was all about how Jesus had all these
            interactions with prostitutes and tax collectors. How
            he loved them just the way they were.

BARBARA: I hope he also mentioned that Jesus didn't think they
            should stay that way.

KIM: Yeah, he did. Somehow he sure got that balance right,
            didn't he?

BARBARA: Who? The pastor or Jesus?

KIM: Jesus!

BARBARA: Just kidding.

KIM: Well, I'm *not* kidding. How do you find a balance
            between not condemning and not condoning?

BARBARA: You ask the best questions!

KIM: So start answering.

BARBARA: I'm glad the sermon was about people encountering
            Jesus. If you ever wanted to start reading the Bible,
            that's where I'd point you—all the places where Jesus
            met people. Like in one of the Gospels. Let me see . . .
            what's a good example? Oh . . . like when a bunch of
            people dragged a woman in front of Jesus. She was
            caught in the act of adultery.

KIM: I think that's what Todd said the pastor talked about.

BARBARA: It's a great story, Kim. You ought to read it. It's in the
            gospel of John.

KIM: I'm almost positive that's what Todd said.

BARBARA: It's like this. Whenever people got close to Jesus, they
            reacted in one of three ways. Either they hated him,
            because he was so holy and they realized they weren't.
            That's like the people who tried to kill him. Being
            near Jesus is like staring into a really bright light. You
            can't take it, so you turn away. Only when it's a person

	who's shining like that, you try to malign him and say he's the one who's bad.
KIM:	Okay.
BARBARA:	The second way people respond when they look at Jesus is . . . mmm, I can't think of a place in the Bible that shows this . . . but I know it happens a lot now People look at Jesus and start thinking they're already like him.
KIM:	Who would say that?
BARBARA:	Nobody actually *says* it. Subconsciously, though, they're thinking, *Well Jesus was loving and accepting, and that's the way I am. I'm never condemning or harsh,* or whatever.
KIM:	But they're not really what they think.
BARBARA:	They can't be. Nobody can. That's where all the hypocrisy comes from that you get so upset about.
KIM:	I'm sorry I keep harping on that.
BARBARA:	Don't be sorry. It *should* bother you that people are self-righteous hypocrites.
KIM:	All right.
BARBARA:	But aren't we all hypocrites some of the time? Maybe even you? Don't you ever fail to live up to your own standards? I'm not even talking about God's standards. I know I sometimes do the exact opposite of what I think I should do.
KIM:	Yeah, you're right.
BARBARA:	That's why the third way of responding to Jesus is the best way. It's accepting him in a humble, I'd say even a broken, way.
KIM:	Is that how that woman responded?
BARBARA:	Who?
KIM:	The one who was dragged in front of Jesus. The one caught in adultery.
BARBARA:	You know, I'm not really sure *how* she responded. I don't think the Bible says. It just says how Jesus didn't

condemn her and then said, "Go and sin no more." I'll look into that. I don't remember if it says what she did.

KIM: I'll bet she *did* respond like you said . . . you know, humble.

BARBARA: I'm with you. I think it must have been really overwhelming for her—I mean she was caught committing a sin. She couldn't deny it.

KIM: Except that it was a trap, wasn't it? Those religious hypocrites who dragged her there—they set it all up. They had to—because where was the man? They should have dragged him in front of Jesus, too, right?

BARBARA: That's true. But that's not an excuse for the woman—it just means that all those men were guilty of sin, too.

KIM: Which is why he told the woman not to sin anymore, because he wanted her to face up to her own sin.

BARBARA: Yes. Which means that even that kind of sin—even sexual sin—is something Jesus is willing to forgive.

KIM: Hmm.

BARBARA: Do you see that, Kim?

KIM: I think so.

BARBARA: When people come to Jesus like that, broken, admitting they've sinned, he accepts them and forgives them, and then he starts changing them. From the inside out. But you've got to see this, Kim. It's only because his death paid for their sins—all of them!

KIM: That sounds good.

BARBARA: It's *very* good.

KIM: Well, maybe next week I'll be able to tell you that I didn't stay in bed on Sunday morning.

BARBARA: I'd love to hear all about it.

KIM: *[Glances at her watch.]* Time to shop, huh?

BARBARA: 'Fraid so.

KIM: What was that tea we had last week? I think I'm going to buy some.

BARBARA: Earl Gray.
KIM: Yeah. I actually think I liked that better than this
            Oolong stuff.
BARBARA: Aisle seven!
KIM: See you next week.

❖

Keep the Conversation Going

* The New Testament book of Ephesians offers important
  perspectives about forgiveness and the difference Christ can
  make in a person's life. The first ten verses of chapter 2 are
  particularly helpful.
* A book with helpful answers to many common questions,
  not just this one about hypocrisy, is Larry Moody and Ken
  Boa, *I'm Glad You Asked* (Colorado Springs: Chariot Victor,
  1995).

144 *apatheism*: *The Atlantic Monthly,* May 2003—http://
    www.theatlantic.com/doc/prem/200305/rauch

154 *Well, I'm against abortion, too, but it's not that simple*:
    It's not that simple! But there are some compassionate
    resources to be found at www.care-net.org. An insightful
    and balanced book, written after interviewing dozens
    of women who had abortions, is Frederica Matthewes-
    Green's *Real Choices: Listening to Women, Looking for
    Alternatives to Abortion* (Ben Lomond, Calif.: Conciliar,
    1997).

160 *But no one goes to the doctor unless he admits he's sick*:
    See Matthew 9:12 and the surrounding context.

164 *dragged a woman in front of Jesus . . . caught in the act
    of adultery:* See John 8:1–11.

In the Cemetery

Pertinent Questions About Life After Death

MILES LINTON WISHES HIS DREAMS WOULD come true. But for the past two months he's awakened every morning with the horrible realization that his dreams are just that—mere escapes for the fleeting hours he is able to sleep. The reality of his waking hours is that he's dying from leukemia. He cries his way through early morning showers as he prepares for every day of teaching. He marvels at the seemingly bottomless reservoir of fluid for his tears as he tries to find answers and strength.

To make matters worse, Miles knows exactly what's going on inside his blood vessels. As a biologist, he's taught the realities and processes of leukemia hundreds of times to his tenth graders at Turnerville High. Those classroom lectures had foreshadowed the explanations the hospital oncologists gave as Miles stared at charts and lab results. He understood the handwriting on the wall long before the men in the white coats opened their mouths.

For the first four months after the initial diagnosis, he struggled to maintain hope. But, recently, discouragement and sadness are winning out as his test results consistently point in the worst possible direction.

"I'm ten for ten," he announced to his wife, Laura, when his last test came back with the same bad news as the previous nine. Cancer. Beyond treatment. Spreading. Laura's tears display more honesty than her husband's sarcasm but both of them feel their optimism eroding with each successive disappointment.

The doctors had stopped discussing options and were now focusing their remarks on timing. Miles has come to accept the inevitable.

His sister, Caryn, also teaches high school science—physics, to be more precise. Always close, Miles and Caryn had traveled rocky paths through their love for science, but had arrived at very different destinations: he to agnostic skepticism, she to Christian faith. Their love for each other had suffered a few bruises over the years as Caryn tried to persuade her brother to embrace the faith she'd found as an adult. Miles's responses ranged from insults to indifference.

Now, as the end approaches, Miles spends hours each day after school sitting on benches in the cemetery. Laura always knows where he'll be after the final class of the day and before he comes home for dinner. Sometimes he reads—philosophy, religion, medical journals, self-help books. In the same way he worked toward a deadline at the end of semesters in college, Miles tries to finish books he merely started years ago—Einstein, Freud, Sartre, and yes, his favorite of all, Gary Larson's *The Complete Far Side*. He can only take so much heaviness!

Lately, he's left the books at home as his concentration and strength wane. Just sitting on benches and thinking is helpful, if not enjoyable.

On a particularly sunny afternoon in early June, Caryn comes to the cemetery to talk to Miles. She approaches him with a mixture of sadness, love, and urgency.

CARYN: Hey, Sailor, come here often?

MILES: I hope you don't use that line anywhere else.

CARYN: How are you doing, Miles?

MILES: Today's a pretty good day.

CARYN: Laura told me I'd find you here.

MILES: I've been coming here a lot lately.

CARYN: Are you okay with that? Isn't this a bit . . . morbid?
MILES: I think of it more as a lab experiment—testing
            the waters, so to speak. I'm going to be here
            permanently pretty soon. So I'm just scoping out the
            neighborhood.
CARYN: Doesn't this bring you down? You were telling me
            how you're practicing positive mental attitude.
            Doesn't this work against that?
MILES: For some reason it doesn't. Besides, the PMA tactics
            only helped for a while. Once that last pathology
            test came back, I needed to shift tactics. Different
            hypothesis—different procedure. That kind of thing.
CARYN: And the different procedure now is . . . what?
MILES: I'm not sure. I've been coming here, right to this
            very bench—lovely spot, isn't it?—and just thinking.
            I've been coming here now for about a month, I
            guess, except when it rains. I feel like I've gotten to
            know some of these people. Well, they're not people
            anymore. But I've imagined who they might have
            been. Look at this one—Juan Dominese, "beloved
            husband and father." Do the math, Caryn. He was
            only thirty-four when he died—forty-seven years ago!
            His kids are now older than he was when he died. I
            just wonder where his kids are now and how they're
            doing and stuff like that.
CARYN: Is that how you've spent most of your time here?
MILES: No. That's a tiny part. No, I've been wondering about
            . . . ahem . . . what comes next, actually. Life after
            death. I've been reexamining a lot of my beliefs.
CARYN: Like which ones?
MILES: Almost all of them. Mostly, I've been thinking about
            science.
CARYN: The love of both of our lives!
MILES: Yes. But a fickle lover she is, don't you think?
CARYN: Tell me more.

MILES: You're one of the few people I can talk to about this. Somehow you've been able to hang on to science as well as your faith. I admire that.

CARYN: But Miles, you know it hasn't always been like this for me.

MILES: You've always loved science . . .

CARYN: Right. But science led me away from faith—for a very long time. Somewhere during college—undergrad days—I felt like I had to make a terrible choice. Either my science professors were right or Mom and Dad and the people at church were right. But they couldn't both be right—or so it seemed. There were all those interminably long arguments about how old the earth was, and was it six literal days that God took to create the world, and all those books Mom and Dad sent to me.

MILES: That seems so long ago, doesn't it?

CARYN: Like billions and billions of years ago.

MILES: Ha! You sound like Carl Sagan.

CARYN: It does feel good to laugh about it now, though.

MILES: And you sided with your science professors.

CARYN: The physicists. It was like I stepped off a diving board and took the plunge and said the scientists were right. The earth is old. The Christians are wrong. And I didn't step foot in a church for another fifteen years.

MILES: Stepping off a diving board. Nice image. Do you remember?

CARYN: Oh, I do remember. How can I forget? I have such great memories of us together at the pool all those summers.

MILES: Me too. That was where I fell in love with water—I guess that had a lot to do with me becoming a biologist. But . . . science led you *away* from believing in God? What brought you back?

CARYN: I didn't say it led me away from belief in God. I said it led me away from faith.

MILES: And the difference is . . . ?

CARYN: All the difference in the world.

MILES: Stop being evasive. I haven't got the time. I'm dying, remember?

CARYN: Yeah. Well, science led me away from a specific kind of faith—a very narrow view of Christianity. I've since found out that it's not the only variety out there. Some scientists, in fact, see no contradiction between their science and their Christian faith.

MILES: And that's what you'd say is true for you now?

CARYN: Yes.

MILES: And what was it that led you to this place?

CARYN: Science!

MILES: Nice. Can you explain?

CARYN: I hope so.

MILES: I do too, because, to tell you the truth, science seems to have failed me.

CARYN: What do you mean?

MILES: I fell in love with science too—also when I was in college.

CARYN: I remember.

MILES: All those trips to the wetlands.

CARYN: And how did science fail you?

MILES: You answer my question first, and then I'll try to answer yours.

CARYN: Okay, but I need to explain this in a certain way. There are two points I want to make: order and music.

MILES: Music?

CARYN: Don't go out of order!

MILES: Sorry.

CARYN: You biologists. I'll start with order. Scientists talk a lot about chaos but there's a whole lot more order to the physical world than disorder.

MILES: Yeah.

CARYN: The more I studied the physical world, the more
             incredible it seemed to me. I kept finding patterns.
             There were connections between creatures living on
             the earth and the earth itself. I kept trying to avoid
             the word *design* but the more I studied—and it wasn't
             just in physics, Miles, it was everywhere—it seemed
             likely that there was a sense of design rather than
             random, purposeless chaos.

MILES: A month ago, I would have argued with you
             vehemently. But after sitting here these past few weeks
             and being honest, I have to consider that you might be
             right.

CARYN: Should I give some examples of this kind of design?

MILES: Nah, I've got a great one growing inside my body.

CARYN: Leukemia?

MILES: In a backward way, yes.

CARYN: This I've got to hear.

MILES: Leukemia is so horrible that it spotlights the good
             way blood usually works—the normal healthy way
             the white cells fight disease. It's amazing. It's got order
             and design written all over it. It's just that sometimes
             things break down—that's what's happening to me.
             But my disease is a horrific distortion of the way
             things are supposed to work.

CARYN: You've been doing a lot of thinking here.

MILES: Does that make sense? I tried explaining it to Laura,
             and she just got mad and started to cry.

CARYN: Yes, this makes sense—but sense isn't what Laura
             needs right now. She needs a miraculous healing for
             you.

MILES: And a shoulder to cry on.

CARYN: I'm trying to be that for her.

MILES: Thanks.

CARYN: I think your backward way of seeing design *does* make
             sense.

MILES: So where does music fit into all this?

CARYN: From a scientific point of view—if all we know is from science—music is nothing more than just vibrations moving air and stimulating parts of our ears and our brains. I've lectured about acoustics and the kids always find it fascinating. But it doesn't explain the whole attraction we have to music. If acoustics and science alone could explain it all, why do we have such emotional responses to Bach's *Brandenburg Concertos* or Rachmaninov's piano concertos?

MILES: Or Coltrane's "Giant Steps"?

CARYN: Exactly.

MILES: I've got to think about this some more.

CARYN: There's a kind of science I really love—the humble kind. And then there's a kind of science—I think you could actually call it "scientism"—that goes beyond what it really should. It claims more than it has a right to.

MILES: "Scientism"—that's a good way to put it. Although there are fewer scientists who believe in scientism than you'd think.

CARYN: I agree. Here's what I've come to love about science. It taught me to examine things and to question them. It made me into someone who questions and even doubts. But it also made me into someone who accepts things, once I see that there's good support for believing them. That applies to God as well.

MILES: You're right. I love that about science, too.

CARYN: And you know what? There's a kind of Christianity I've come to love also—a humble kind. One that has a beautiful message. One that doesn't try to say more than it should.

MILES: Like what?

CARYN: Before we get into all that, I want to know why you said that science was a fickle lover.

MILES: She promises more than she can deliver.

CARYN: Go on.

MILES: Science can be so arrogant.

CARYN: Don't you mean that some *scientists* can be arrogant?

MILES: Thank you. That's a helpful corrective. Some scientists claim that the only way we can know anything is through empirical scientific discovery. I used to believe that. Shoot, I used to teach that. And who knows how many high school kids believed me without question. But I've come to see that we were cutting off the branch we were sitting on.

CARYN: What do you mean?

MILES: We have the nerve to say, "The only way we can know anything is through empirical scientific discovery." But how can we know that? That statement can't be empirically scientifically proven!

CARYN: But science, I mean scientists, don't have to be arrogant.

MILES: I know—at least *now* I know.

CARYN: I've found that the best science is truly humble. It's willing to say what we do know and what we don't know. Take the best journal articles, for example. They add their little piece of discovery to the body of accepted scientific knowledge, and the writers are willing to allow others to verify or correct or add more.

MILES: And what about this religion you mentioned that's not humble?

CARYN: Do you remember that speaker who came to our high school? The one who made you so mad.

MILES: The guy with the comb-over?

CARYN: I don't remember what his hair was like. He talked about Genesis.

MILES: That's the one. He said that you must be either a Christian and believe in a young earth or be an atheist and believe in an old earth.

CARYN: He's Exhibit A for this kind of arrogant Christian.

MILES: But wasn't he right—in a sense? If science is right about the age of the earth then isn't Genesis wrong?

CARYN: That's what I thought for a lot of years.

MILES: You don't think that anymore?

CARYN: No.

MILES: What changed?

CARYN: I read the first chapter of Genesis again—and I started reading a lot of commentaries.

MILES: Why?

CARYN: I went to a physics conference, and there was an informal gathering of Christians who met there over breakfast.

MILES: It was a conference for Christian physicists?

CARYN: No, not at all. It was purely a scientific conference— the American Institute of Physics. There were like five hundred people there. But this breakfast was just for Christians who wanted to get together.

MILES: How many people came to this breakfast?

CARYN: Take a guess.

MILES: Ten? A dozen?

CARYN: Almost a hundred!

MILES: Really?

CARYN: Really. And they weren't stupid. I picked up some of their literature but couldn't stay very long. I did meet a few of them, though, and I was impressed. They were very different than the comb-over guy, and I wanted to find out more.

MILES: And you did a lot of reading. What did you find out?

CARYN: Genesis is *not* a science textbook. And it's not even a history book—although I *do* believe that what it says really did happen. But it's not written like history— the first chapter, at least. It's really quite poetic.

MILES: Like a myth.

CARYN: No, at least not the way the word *myth* has evolved.

When people use the word myth, they usually mean
something fanciful and probably not true—and
whether it's true or not doesn't matter all that much.
But Genesis doesn't read like myth, and if it's not true,
that *does* matter.

MILES: How so?

CARYN: It claims to be true. And lots of other places in the
Bible refer back to it as true. Jesus even affirmed it. If
it's not true, the whole Bible is on shaky ground.

MILES: Go on.

CARYN: But I wouldn't call it history per se. I'm not totally
sure of what to call it.

MILES: Theology?

CARYN: Kind of. But it doesn't read like a theology book. It's
a beautiful, poetic, introduction to the whole book of
Genesis.

MILES: Maybe like an overture? At the beginning of one of
those old-fashioned musicals.

CARYN: That's not bad—but it has a worshipful tone to it.
What I'm trying to say is that the genre of literature of
Genesis chapter 1 has to be taken into account when
you interpret it. You can't demand the level of techni-
cal specifics you would of a scientific journal article.

MILES: But it's still truthful and historically accurate.

CARYN: Yes. But it's much more concerned with who did the
creating rather than how he did it or how long it took
him. It's supposed to elicit praise and obedience not a
calendar or a timetable.

MILES: But what about those six literal days? "And it was
evening and it was morning, the first day." That sure
sounds like twenty-four-hour time periods.

CARYN: Yes, it does. And I think the mentioning of evening
and morning points to a twenty-four-hour period of
time. But it doesn't say, "the first day."

MILES: Yes, it does!

CARYN: Look it up in the most literal translations. Or look carefully at the footnotes. The *New American Standard Bible* gets it right. It literally says, "There was evening and there was morning, one day." The other days say, "second, third, fourth," etc. But the so-called "first" one doesn't say first.

MILES: And how do you interpret that?

CARYN: I'm not sure. It could mean several things.

MILES: Like?

CARYN: It could mean that what took place on that particular day was a long time after "In the beginning."

MILES: I think I've heard of this. Don't some people talk about a "gap theory"?

CARYN: Yes, but there're a lot of variations on that theme. How long the gap is, when the gap is, whether it was in between Genesis 1:1 and 1:2 or somewhere else. I'm not sure which variation you've heard about.

MILES: So the earth could be a lot older if there's a long time gap between 1:1 and "one day."

CARYN: Sure.

MILES: And how old do these gap-theory people think the earth is?

CARYN: Wait a minute. The gap theory is only one possible explanation. There are a lot of people who hold to a wide array of theories. The point that I'm trying to make is that Genesis 1 isn't interested in just timing. It's interested in who did all this amazing creating. When's the last time you read Genesis 1?

MILES: Probably when I was sitting there listening to the comb-over guy—thirty years ago.

CARYN: Might be time to dust it off again. Bring it here some day and just enjoy it. Let it tell you the things it's trying to emphasize instead of reading a scientific agenda into it. Look at the things it repeats: "And God said . . . and it was so," "And God said . . . and it was so." "And it was good." "And it was good." "And it was good." Do you see what it's trying to say?

MILES: God only has to say words to create things, and what he creates turns out pretty darn good.

CARYN: Precisely. And the people who first heard these things were being encouraged to pay attention to God's words.

MILES: Isn't there some other set of reasons why Christians think the earth is young? Something about adding up ages of people?

CARYN: Some Christians think that. I'm not sure of all their reasoning. Some of them add up ages of generations, but the Bible never claims to have an exhaustive list of people. So to add up ages could be missing entire centuries of people.

MILES: There must be other reasons they came up with an age of the earth being about ten thousand years.

CARYN: Oh, you're such a scientist! Leaving no stone unturned! If the Bible was concerned about the age of the earth, it would have told us in ways that wouldn't require a calculator. I just don't think the age of the earth is all that big a deal.

MILES: I doubt it's all that big a deal to scientists either!

CARYN: I think you're right, Miles. I've gone to a lot of conferences for physicists, and there just isn't much talk about how old the earth is. I have this dream about a certain crowd of people. Someday they're going to get to heaven, and they'll ask God how old the earth is, and he'll scratch his head and say, "What does that matter?" And I don't think there'll be many serious scientists in that particular crowd, or many serious students of Genesis, either!

MILES: I wonder what Mr. Comb-over would say to you about this?

CARYN: Do you want to know what Galileo said? "The Bible tells us how to go to heaven, not how the heavens go."

MILES: Galileo! Now *there's* a guy who got himself into trouble with the church.

CARYN: I'm sorry I brought him into this. Yes, he did get himself into trouble—with the church—at that time. The church made some huge mistakes. I won't defend them. But don't throw out the whole of Christianity just because of that particular sub-group's mistakes.

MILES: That wouldn't be good science, now, would it?

CARYN: Thank you.

MILES: Listen, Caryn—I'm looking for something more . . . I'm not sure of the right word . . . certainty, maybe. Are you absolutely certain that there's a God? Or do you have confidence that your faith is valid?

CARYN: Those are two very different questions, Miles. And you've got a bunch of terms that need some defining—Certain? Confidence? Valid?

MILES: I'm trying to think out loud with you. Go easy on me—we're in a cemetery, not a laboratory.

CARYN: Right. I'll start with your first question—"Am I absolutely certain that there's a God?" No. But I am very confident that he exists. Do you see the difference?

MILES: I think so.

CARYN: Absolute certainty is a category we inherited from Descartes or some other enlightenment thinkers. And a lot of scientists latched onto certainty like it was the new messiah. I'm not so sure we should have fallen for such arrogance.

MILES: Arrogance?

CARYN: That we can know anything with absolute certainty? Yeah, I'd say that's arrogant.

MILES: What about all those people, friends of Mom and

Dad, who used to say that little ditty, "I know that I know that I know . . ."

CARYN: I don't even know what that means.

MILES: So sometimes you doubt God's existence?

CARYN: That's too far on the other end of the spectrum. Somewhere in between absolute certainty and doubt is a very reasonable confidence. It's closer to the certainty side of things—just not a hundred percent.

MILES: I'm actually relieved to hear this.

CARYN: I was, too, when I first met people who talked about their faith this way. It's actually ironic—when you insist on absolute one-hundred percent certainty, you end up doubting everything. But if you aim for confidence, you're likely to get just that—confidence. And it's a whole lot more enjoyable being confident than cynical.

MILES: I think I see what you mean. Insisting on absolute proof is an all-or-nothing deal. And you usually end up with nothing.

CARYN: Usually? If you end up on the other side of things you end up with cocky arrogance, thinking that science . . . uh, scientists, can solve everything.

MILES: Back when I was in college I went to one of those debates between an atheist and a Christian held on campus. I really wanted the atheist to win—but he *was* cocky. At one point he said, "Science is just a few years away from solving every problem we have in our society." Can you imagine?

CARYN: Amazing.

MILES: There was this loud gasp from the audience. Even *I* thought that was lunacy.

CARYN: Most scientists aren't that sure of themselves—or their disciplines.

MILES: I know. But I didn't finish the story. Right after the atheist said that, and everybody gasped, some guy

behind me said real loud, "Praise God!" The place
went hysterical.

CARYN: Ha! That *is* funny.

MILES: I wasn't laughing at the time. But now I think it's
funny.

CARYN: What changed?

MILES: I don't know. That's a good question. I guess I'm
seeing that we scientists hold some things by faith
too. We have to. We make reasonable assertions based
on what we're pretty sure of. But there's always this
sense—well, not always—but the best scientists have
a posture of, "It seems reasonable to assert . . ."

CARYN: That's right. And I think that's what the best of
Christianity claims. It's far more reasonable—there,
I'll even go that far—it's more *reasonable* to believe
that God does exist than to believe we're in a
purposeless, un-designed, random universe.

MILES: That's actually a pretty bold statement as it stands.
And it's not that "I know that I know that I know"
blather.

CARYN: Miles, maybe you're not up for doing any more
reading given your . . . your . . . situation . . .

MILES: *[whispering in a joking manner]* It's okay to say it here.
No one's listening . . . everyone around here is dead
already.

CARYN: It is kind of awkward to say certain words . . . but if
you can joke about it . . .

MILES: Sometimes.

CARYN: What I was going to say is if you're interested, some
new things are being written by scientists that support
what I'm trying to say. They're taking a scientific
approach—a humble one—toward the whole issue of
the existence of God, and they're coming out of the
closet as theists. A lot of them talk about something
called "the anthropic principle."

MILES: I've heard of this.

CARYN: It simply says there's a lot to our world that seems like
           it was made with the intent of supporting human life.
           In a sense, it's so unlikely that there'd be just the right
           amount of oxygen, just the right temperature, just the
           right atmospheric pressure, just the right of a lot of
           other things to make human life possible. They like to
           talk about a "privileged planet."

MILES: I like that. I might like to read some of these things.
           Do you have any condensed abstracts?

CARYN: I'll see what I can find.

MILES: How does all this about certainty and confidence
           relate to the proofs for God's existence?

CARYN: I know—I learned a lot about what Anselm and
           Aquinas and others said when they tried to prove
           God's existence. I don't know if they felt like they'd
           succeeded or if their case was overstated by others. I
           don't think we can prove God's existence. But I don't
           think that's a big problem.

MILES: Really?

CARYN: I don't think it's a deal breaker. Some people say,
           "You can't prove God's existence," as if that's some
           final roadblock to the question. But it's not. I can still
           believe in God—I can still believe that it's the most
           reasonable explanation of our situation—without
           insisting that I can prove his existence.

MILES: Do you tell this to your students?

CARYN: Are you kidding? I need the paycheck. Only if they
           ask me outside of class. You know how people would
           respond if I talked about this in the classroom?
           Atheists can be amazingly religious about insisting on
           the separation of church and state.

MILES: Let's not get into that.

CARYN: Right. Miles, I'm not trying to prove to you that God
           exists. I'm simply saying that a lot of scientists take

	a theistic approach, and it seems a more reasonable insight about the way the world is—how it works and our place in the universe.
MILES:	This is really refreshing. I'm sorry it took leukemia to make me willing to listen to you.
CARYN:	Don't be too hard on yourself.
MILES:	I wasn't exactly hostile toward religion. I was just indifferent. I used to think of churches the way I thought about the Petsmart store.
CARYN:	Should I be insulted by that?
Miles.	No. You know what I mean—the Petsmart place.
CARYN:	The place they sell dog food and cat food and things for your pets?
MILES:	Right. I don't have any pets.
CARYN:	That's funny. A biologist without pets.
MILES:	I think I got tired of cleaning up after them. We used to have a dog, but after the kids came and there were all those diapers—
CARYN:	Got it.
MILES:	Anyway, the Petsmart store is just something that's totally irrelevant to my life. I don't mean that in a condemning way. Just neutral. I think that's how I thought about churches, too.
CARYN:	Interesting analogy. I wonder how many other people think the same way.
MILES:	I don't know, but all of a sudden I've got a pet.
CARYN:	Huh?
MILES:	My pet leukemia. It barks all the time and tells me to feed it—with answers about life after death. I never thought I needed those kinds of answers . . . until now.
CARYN:	Maybe you're lucky.
MILES:	No one's said *that* to me in the past year.
CARYN:	I'm sorry . . . what I meant was—
MILES:	It's okay. I know you're on my side. But why do you say I'm lucky?

CARYN: All of us have the need to know about life after
           death. We've all got that dog, so to speak. Yours just
           barks loud enough to hear it. Most people ignore the
           barking within them.

MILES: Hmm.

CARYN: It's like that time, at the pool, when the lifeguard
           rescued you but you weren't really drowning.

MILES: I'm not following.

CARYN: You remember the time I'm talking about?

MILES: Oh sure. I was dog paddling around in the deep
           end of the pool and he thought I was drowning. So
           he dove in and put me in a cross-chest carry, and
           towed me to the side of the pool and asked if I was
           all right.

CARYN: [*laughing*] I remember you telling us later that you
           wanted to ask him if *he* was all right.

MILES: Yeah. I'm still not following what this has to do with
           death.

CARYN: Christianity offers to save people. But a lot of people
           don't think they're drowning, so they wonder why
           they need to be saved.

MILES: We're puzzled about even more than that, Caryn. We
           wonder what's wrong with all of you lifeguards. You
           tell us we're drowning when it seem to us we're just
           dog paddling and enjoying the water.

CARYN: I see your point.

MILES: But, you know what? This time, I might really *be*
           drowning.

CARYN: That's why I said you were lucky.

MILES: Lucky to be drowning?

CARYN: Lucky to have something *show* you that you're
           drowning—in a way you can't deny.

MILES: I don't know. This is tough to handle.

CARYN: I understand.

MILES: Would you like to walk a little? I sometimes sit on

	another bench on the other side of the cemetery. It's got a nice view of the sun when it's setting.
CARYN:	Sure.
MILES:	I like what you said about believing that God exists— that it's "reasonable" instead of absolutely proved.
CARYN:	I'm convinced there's a cumulative case in favor of believing in God. I'm not sure that any one piece of evidence seals the deal. But when you add them all up, it's pretty compelling.
MILES:	But which god are you talking about? Do you remember what Einstein said about his belief in God? He said he believed in Spinoza's god, not a personal one.
CARYN:	I can't blame him.
MILES:	You think he was right?
CARYN:	Oh, not at all.
MILES:	I'm begging you, Caryn—I have no time for dramatic presentations.
CARYN:	I'm not trying to be dramatic, Miles. Einstein's god and Spinoza's god are a whole lot more appealing to lots of people than the one in the Bible. Maybe appealing is the wrong word. Those gods are certainly a lot more . . . comfortable.
MILES:	Go on.
CARYN:	An impersonal god, or god in the pantheistic sense, makes no demands on us. It—he . . . she, the force, whatever's the best way to refer to that kind of god— makes us feel good or empowered. But the God of the Bible is a holy, consuming fire. Who wants that?
MILES:	Apparently, you.
CARYN:	Yes. But not because it makes me feel comfortable.
MILES:	Then what does this God do for you?
CARYN:	Can I take a little time to answer that? I don't have a cute sound bite ready as a response.
MILES:	You're among friends.

CARYN: When I'm doing those units on acoustics in my
           physics class, I bring in a couple of tuning forks of
           the same size. I show how tuning forks of the same
           frequency cause each other to vibrate.

MILES: Do you use one of those amplifying boxes—to make
           the sound louder?

CARYN: Right. I make one fork vibrate by hitting it, and then
           I put it on the amplifying box—and without even
           touching the other tuning fork, the sound of the first
           one makes the second one start vibrating.

MILES: Got it.

CARYN: God is like the ultimate tuning fork. He awakens the
           frequency within me. His frequency is in tune with
           the truest inner frequency in me.

MILES: Can you be a little bit more concrete?

CARYN: Einstein's god or Spinoza's god is an impersonal force.
           But I'm *not* an impersonal force. Other gods don't
           communicate. But I *do*. I'm out of frequency with a
           vague, impersonal, pantheistic god. Something inside
           me cries out for knowing a personal, communicating,
           loving God. Any other kind of god seems alien to
           what I am.

MILES: Did you just *mean* to say "what I am" instead of "who
           I am"?

CARYN: I meant both.

MILES: How does having *your* kind of God make you feel
           uncomfortable then?

CARYN: There's something about this God—the God the Bible
           talks about—that resonates with me. That's the word
           I was looking for—resonates. He's a good God. He's
           a holy God. *So* good and holy that something in me
           also tells me I can't connect with this God because of
           things in me that don't belong in his presence.

MILES: You say something inside you resonates with this
           God. What do you think that is?

CARYN: Something that's just . . . well. . . . When I look at
           the world, at nature—your world, Miles, the animal
           kingdom—if that was all I had to observe in my
           laboratory, I wouldn't come up with the idea that
           there was a good or loving god in the universe.

MILES: Why not?

CARYN: There's so much evil in the world . . . so many animals
           kill other animals with such violence. Look at how
           insects catch their prey and devour them. It's gross.
           And look at all the pain in the world—earthquakes
           and violent storms. How in the world did people ever
           come up with the notion that the God who exists is
           a good or loving God? It seems the *visible* evidence
           points more in the exact opposite direction.

MILES: And yet we do come up with that kind of God,
           don't we?

CARYN: Yes. And I think we do because something inside of
           us was planted there to find fulfillment in just such a
           God.

MILES: I'm not so sure.

CARYN: I realize I'm throwing a lot at you. Maybe we should
           take a break.

MILES: I don't need a break. Keep going. I'm just not sure that
           I can believe all that you're saying.

CARYN: I'd be surprised if you did. I'm saying things that are
           the exact opposite of what you've believed for a long
           time.

MILES: True. But I'm also reexamining those very things. So I
           don't mind a little questioning of my hypotheses.

CARYN: Here's another way to look at it. Maybe we don't have
           an airtight argument or an airtight proof—but maybe
           we have an airtight Person.

MILES: That sounds cute, but I'm not sure what you mean.

CARYN: The design that I see in the world points me toward
           God. But it's only a pointer. And the way your blood

is *supposed* to work, that's also a pointer. Death is a pointer. It may be the most potent one we've got. Death is a painful reminder that we're meant for another world. But we need more than pointers if we're going to get the answers we're hungering for.

MILES: Keep going.

CARYN: Sooner or later, if this is ever going to make any sense, we've got to see where all the pointers point.

MILES: And that is where?

CARYN: It's not where—it's who. They point to Jesus.

MILES: I knew he was going to end up in this conversation.

CARYN: You sound disappointed.

MILES: He was always used like a trump card whenever I talked about God or life or religion. But it seemed to me like someone was pulling a rabbit out of a hat. What does *he* have to do with what we've been talking about?

CARYN: I know what you mean. When we were growing up in church, it did seem like Jesus was used that way in an argument.

MILES: I'm not anti-Jesus, Caryn. I just haven't seen how he fits.

CARYN: Let me see if I can make him fit. That sounds horrible—let me see if I can *show* how he fits.

MILES: Before you do, I really need to say something. I realize that when we've talked about this before, sometimes I was a jerk. I just wanted to get you to shut up. I know that, and I'm sorry. I hope you forgive me. Can we pretend that those discussions—arguments, really—never took place? I'm really listening this time.

CARYN: Yes. We can forget those . . . you're right, they were arguments.

MILES: You remember that time at Thanksgiving?

CARYN: [*winking*] No, I don't remember.

MILES: Thanks.

CARYN: Okay. New discussion. Let's start here. Jesus was
           smart.
MILES: That's a different place to start.
CARYN: I know. But when that thought hit me, it completely
           changed my perspective. It makes sense, doesn't it?
           If Jesus is who Christians say he is—the God of the
           universe who took on the form of a human being—
           then he has to be smart—brilliant even. He has to
           be the smartest person who ever lived. Smarter than
           Einstein and Beethoven and whoever else you think
           was a genius.
MILES: This is good.
CARYN: And what he said about life is worth listening to.
           Better yet, what he said about life after death is
           absolutely crucial to listen to.
MILES: And what did he say?
CARYN: He said he's the key to getting eternal life.
MILES: The key?
CARYN: No, I'm sorry. He's the door.
MILES: How so?
CARYN: By his death.
MILES: C'mon, Caryn. This is no time for being cryptic.
CARYN: Listen, if all I look at about Jesus is his teaching about
           loving one another, I miss the main point. He's more
           than a great teacher and a great example. Sure, he's
           both of those things. But he's also a great substitute.
           He's the ultimate substitute.
MILES: He died in our place, right?
CARYN: Right.
MILES: I never really understood that. Why did he have to die
           in our place?
CARYN: All right. Let's try it like this. Let's say you're standing
           next to train tracks and a train is coming. And you're
           with a friend. Right as the train comes, this friend
           says to you, "Let me show you how much I love you,"

and he jumps in front of the train and gets killed. What are you thinking?

MILES: He obviously didn't know about my latest lab results.

CARYN: Okay ... but ... you can be so difficult sometimes. You know what I mean. Suppose you were healthy and he did that.

MILES: I'd think this guy had a problem.

CARYN: Right.

MILES: Really? I thought you were going to say that's what Jesus did for me. And that makes no sense to me at all.

CARYN: I know. And that's how a lot of people think of Jesus' death. If that were the *good* way to think about it, then Jesus had some serious problems.

MILES: And you're saying there's another way to think about this.

CARYN: Yes. Suppose you're standing on the train tracks and the train comes. And your friend pushes you out of the way to save your life but he gets killed in the process. He died so you didn't have to.

MILES: So the oncoming train is death?

CARYN: Hmm. Not exactly.

MILES: Because we're all going to die anyway—even if we accept Jesus' death in our place, right?

CARYN: Right.

MILES: I still don't get it.

CARYN: Let me try again. There's no perfect illustration. That oncoming train—it's not just physical death. You're right. We all experience that.

MILES: Tell me about it.

CARYN: Let's try this. Do you remember when Jesus was praying before he was arrested? He said, "Let this cup pass from me." Do you remember?

MILES: Yes.

CARYN: What cup was he talking about? Better yet, what was *in* the cup?

MILES: Ah . . . I'm not sure . . . was he talking about the cross?
           He was asking not to have to go to the cross?

CARYN: Kind of. But there's more to it. In the Bible, see, lots
           of times a cup was a symbol of God's judgment. Jesus
           was asking for God's *judgment* to pass by him.

MILES: God's judgment of what?

CARYN: Of people's sins. Other people's sins. All of God's
           judgment for sin was a pretty heavy burden for Jesus
           to bear. Not his own but the sins of all the people that
           he was about to die for.

MILES: Because . . . ?

CARYN: Because somebody has to pay for sin.

MILES: Why?

CARYN: That's the reality of sin and forgiveness. Whenever
           someone sins—and there's a need for forgiveness—
           somebody pays. Either the person who sinned or the
           person who does the forgiving.

MILES: Can you give me an example?

CARYN: Just a few minutes ago, you apologized to me for
           being a jerk when we had some discussions about
           Christ. Right?

MILES: Right.

CARYN: And I forgave you. I chose not to make you pay for
           that sin against me. I could have made you pay—with
           isolation from me, or with insults from me, or
           some other way. I could insist you do something to
           reconnect us. That's paying for sin.

MILES: You could have made me grovel.

CARYN: That's a form of payment. But in this case, I chose to
           forgive you. Which means I paid for your sin.

MILES: How?

CARYN: I paid for it by giving up my right to get revenge of
           some kind.

MILES: I don't know if this illustration is working for me, but
           I think I know what you're trying to say. Last summer

another teacher in the science department cheated me out of a deal where I'd get to teach the honors' bio class. He lied and really screwed me over. When I finally decided to let it go and not make him pay for that, it was like I was paying for his sin.

CARYN: Good. I'm glad you came up with that example.

MILES: I think I get it. Somebody pays for sin—somehow.

CARYN: Right. But when it comes to our sin against God, his payment is much bigger than we realize.

MILES: Bigger?

CARYN: When I asked you what was in that cup that Jesus eventually drank—it was God's holy wrath against sin. That kind of wrath—and what Jesus did for us— is hard for us to grasp, but our escaping that wrath means a lot more than just being forgiven for a few mistakes.

MILES: So you're saying that I'm pond scum and God's a lot greater than we think.

CARYN: He *is* a lot greater—and a lot more perfect and holy and righteous than we think. But I don't think pond scum is a good analogy.

MILES: Why not?

CARYN: Pond scum seems so impersonal. It *is* impersonal. But we're persons—we're created in God's image. So our rebelling against God is a lot worse than pond scum simply mutating in some bad way.

MILES: You're saying that he's our Creator and we treat him like crap.

CARYN: You're getting closer. There are two sides to this story. There's our response to him—we treat him like crap, to use your words—and his response to us—he treats us like children despite our rebellion.

MILES: I'm really trying not to react the way I always have when I hear this talk about God paying for our sin.

CARYN: Good. And I'm trying to put it in different ways so

           you can get past some of the clichés you've heard a million times.

MILES: I think that's a good approach.

CARYN: How's this: The One who created us experienced "un-creation" for us so we could be recreated.

MILES: Did you just make that up?

CARYN: No. I heard it in a sermon somewhere.

MILES: Say that again.

CARYN: The One who created us experienced "un-creation" for us so we could be recreated.

MILES: "Un-creation"?

CARYN: He was undone. He experienced the death we should have died. He was torn apart so we could be put together. Are any of these working?

MILES: I think so.

CARYN: Miles, I feel like I owe you a big apology.

MILES: For what?!

CARYN: All these years I've talked to you about God and Christ and it was like a cold, hard, lab report.

MILES: What do you mean?

CARYN: I kept sending you articles about archeological discoveries, papers delivered by philosophers, intellectual arguments for the Christian worldview.

MILES: I didn't mind all that much.

CARYN: But it was like I was clubbing you over the head. But what's worst, I was ignoring something more important.

MILES: Like . . . ?

CARYN: I was so concerned about trying to convince you that Christianity is *true,* I forgot to tell you it's *good.*

MILES: I'm not sure I would have heard that message, either.

CARYN: It's not just a message. Yeah, I wanted you to believe the message—the true message. But I also wanted you to experience the reality of Christ—a very good reality. It's true—but it's also very good. When I emphasized just the true part, though, it probably came off sounding like an argument, and that certainly couldn't have felt very good to you.

MILES: Don't be so hard on yourself, Caryn. You showed me that your faith was good. Plenty of times.

CARYN: Really? How?

MILES: I could tell it was your faith in Christ that shaped the way your whole family related to each other. It helped your marriage. It helped you and Joe raise your girls—they're pretty impressive young women.

CARYN: I'm not so sure you'd say that if you were at our place this morning.

MILES: Stop. Kids can be a pain—and I'm sure your girls are no angels. But there's a kind of love in your house that I notice. Laura and I remark about it every time we're together with you guys. You don't see it. But we do.

CARYN: Thanks.

MILES: You've been a great sister.

CARYN: I just wish I could have made our interaction about Christ not so . . . I don't know the right word . . . clinical . . . dry, academic.

MILES: Do you think I would have responded any differently if you had?

CARYN: I guess you're right. I just remember that, for me, it wasn't just the intellectual arguments that persuaded me to believe. It was the people I met at our church. It was a community.

MILES: You've been there now for a long time, haven't you?

CARYN: Yes. And the thing is, we went there for a long time before I ever made any conscious decisions to believe what they believed. I belonged before I believed.

MILES: That's great.

CARYN: I wish I would've invited you to join us.

MILES: You don't think I actually would've accepted that invitation, do you?

CARYN: A girl can hope, can't she?

MILES: Quit beating up on yourself. That's one part of my
              Positive Mental Attitude routine that does help me.
              Don't blame yourself for things that aren't your fault.
              It's not your fault that I didn't become a Christian.

CARYN: I know.

MILES: Besides, you're doing a pretty good job right now of
              making me think.

CARYN: Better late than never!

MILES: Hey, listen. Laura's making dinner and I need to get
              back home—but I'd like a little time by myself before
              I go. Do you mind if I take a walk now by myself?

CARYN: Not at all.

MILES: I have this routine when I leave here. I walk around
              that corner and go past this one particular grave.
              Eleanor Lovette. She lived two days past her one-
              hundredth birthday! She's kind of an inspiration
              for me.

CARYN: It's nice to see you smile when you say that.

MILES: Uh . . . wait a minute. I have a confession to make.

CARYN: Uh-oh!

MILES: That whole thing about the lifeguard who saved me—
              when I really wasn't drowning.

CARYN: Yeah . . .

MILES: I really was.

CARYN: What?

MILES: At least, I was having some real trouble. I swallowed
              some water and was choking, and he heard me.

CARYN: I can't believe this. You came back to our blanket so
              mad at him. You were ranting and raving about what
              a lunatic he was and how he almost drowned you.

MILES: I was scared.

CARYN: Oh my . . .

MILES: And I was embarrassed.

CARYN: This is amazing.

MILES: I was too proud to admit I really *was* in trouble. And
            when I told you all about it and you sided with me . . .
            that made it even harder to admit the truth.
CARYN: That makes sense.
MILES: Yeah. But it doesn't make it right. I'm sorry.
CARYN: It's okay.
MILES: I had to set the record straight.
CARYN: Another case of better late than never.
MILES: Precisely.

❖

Keep the Conversation Going

* Several of the Psalms talk about God's creative power—
  Psalms 8; 19; 24; 46; 93; 104; and 139.
* Two very helpful books about the specific issue of evolution
  are the following:

Michael Behe, *Darwin's Black Box* (New York: Touchstone,
    1996).
Philip E. Johnson, *Darwin on Trial* (Downers Grove, Ill.:
    InterVarsity, 1993).

174   *music is nothing more than just vibrations*: See John
      Polkinghorne, *Belief in God in an Age of Science* (New
      Haven: Yale University Press, 1998), 18.

176   *I read the first chapter of Genesis again*: See, especially,
      Bruce K. Waltke, *Genesis: A Commentary* (Grand
      Rapids: Zondervan, 2001), 73–78.

177   *But what about those six literal days?*: Helpful insights
      about this divisive issue can be found at www.reasons
      .org.

180   *Do you want to know what Galileo said?*: A helpful
      discussion about Galileo can be found in Denis

Alexander's *Rebuilding the Matrix* (Grand Rapids: Zondervan, 2001), 108–124.

Are you absolutely certain that there's a God?: See Lesslie Newbigin, *Proper Confidence: Faith, Doubt, and Certainty in Christian Discipleship* (Grand Rapids: Eerdmans, 1995).

181　*Science is just a few years away from solving every problem we have in our society*: This is a direct quote of Peter W. Atkins during a debate with William Lane Craig held on April 3, 1998. You can find an audio recording at http://www.leaderu.com/offices/billcraig/docs/craig-atkins.html.

182　*the anthropic principle*: See William A. Dembski, *The Design Revolution: Answering the Toughest Questions About Intelligent Design* (Downers Grove, Ill.: InterVarsity, 2004).

183　*privileged planet*: See www.privilegedplanet.com.

Some people say, "You can't prove God's existence": A very helpful guide is Gregory E. Ganssle's *Thinking About God: First Steps in Philosophy* (Downers Grove, Ill.: InterVarsity, 2004).

186　*What Einstein said about his belief in God?*: Alice Calaprice, *The New Quotable Einstein* (Princeton: Princeton University Press, 2005), 197.

An impersonal god, or god in the pantheistic sense, makes no demands on us: See C. S. Lewis, *Miracles* (New York: Macmillan, 1960), 94.

188　*Maybe we don't have an airtight argument or an airtight proof—but maybe we have an airtight Person*: Again, I am indebted to the teaching of Dr. Tim Keller, pastor of Redeemer Presbyterian Church in New York. Many of the analogies used in this chapter come from his messages. See especially "How Can

I Know God?" by Dr. Tim Keller. You can read the entire paper at www.redeemer2.com/resources/index.cfm?fuseaction=tkeller. There are other valuable resources at www.redeemer.com.

190   *He's the door*: See John 10:1–21 (some translations use "gate" instead of "door").

191   *Let this cup pass from me*: See Matthew 26:39 KJV.

Caryn Martine's Eulogy for Her Brother Miles

FOUR WEEKS AFTER MILES AND CARYN'S graveside chat, Miles slipped into a coma and died. On July 17, Turnerville comes to a collective stillness, and mourners pack Grace Community Church's sanctuary. They'd traveled to honor the life of the high school biology teacher they had come to love. Former students came home from college. Nurses and doctors took the afternoon off. Neighbors carpooled to the service.

Friends, fellow teachers, and relatives listen to Miles's thirteen-year-old daughter, Sandra, play a Chopin prelude on the piano while latecomers find seats. They read the program designed for the service and wipe their eyes. Miles's photo on the cover is full of life, unlike the gaunt image people had visited in the hospital during his last days. To some, the presence of a Bible verse in the program is a surprise. Others find the reference an affirmation of rumors that had recently circulated.

Romans 8:38–39 somehow brings smiles amidst the tears—"For I am convinced that neither death nor life, neither angels nor demons, neither the present nor the future, nor any powers, neither height nor depth, nor anything else in all creation, will be able to separate us from the love of God that is in Christ Jesus our Lord."

The pastor of Grace Community welcomes everyone. Several people speak kind words. Miles's department chairman recounts an exemplary career. Former students reminisce how they fell in love with science as a result of tenth-grade biology. Miles's children speak of the love of a father who took them on vacations, helped them with homework, and "always won in tickle fights."

Laura, Miles's wife, chooses not to speak, fearing she'll break down and dim the atmosphere she hopes will prevail that day—one of gratitude for Miles's life and friendship. She hugs each speaker as they descend from the platform but stays out of the limelight as much as possible.

Caryn Martine, Miles's sister, stands out as the most memorable speaker of the service. Summoning a sense of serenity that originates from within, she steps to the podium. Crumpled tissue in hand, she stands motionless for a second, occasioning a pause and allowing everyone to focus.

"Thank you so much for being here today," she begins. "It means a lot to me and to our family that we're not going through this alone. Just your very presence makes a difference. I've been asked by Laura, my sister-in-law, to be our family spokesperson and say a few words about Miles.

"But before I do that, I want to extend a special word of thanks to a group of wonderful people who took time off to come today. Seated on my right are a handful of nurses and doctors who took care of Miles in the oncology unit at Turnerville Hospital. You people have a very difficult job but you do it so well. You helped Miles so much during these past few weeks. You eased a lot of his pain and were patient with explaining things to him and to us. Thank you for taking such good care of my brother.

"I wish you all could have known Miles the way I did. None of you could have known him for as long as I did. I'm his older sister, and I welcomed him into our home when he was a newborn. I actually do remember the day my parents brought him home from the hospital. I was so proud to be the older sister and have someone to take care of. I sat on our living room couch and held him in my arms. I remember saying, 'Hi, baby Miles. You have such a beautiful head.'

"Little did I know, years later, I'd be sitting in a hospital room, holding him in my arms again and stroking the hair on that beautiful head. Little did I know that, even though he was younger than me, he would take care of me far more than I would protect and raise him.

"My favorite memory is from a time when I was about twelve and Miles was only eight. It was at our neighborhood pool. On this particular afternoon, I decided I was going to jump off the high dive. I'd never ventured to do it but I made up my mind that I wasn't going to be outdone by my little brother. That summer, Miles had just reached the height of forty-eight inches—the required height in order to go off the high dive. Miles had done it for the first time the day before, and all that night, he made fun of me for being a chicken. I swore I wouldn't sit through another humiliating dinner. I was going to overcome my fear and take the plunge.

"I waited in line for what seemed like hours. Then I climbed the five hundred steps [or so it seemed] and got to the end of the board . . . and froze. I just couldn't do it. People from the line below me started yelling at me to jump. People in the pool started laughing. Even the old ladies who played cards under the oak trees were staring at me. The lifeguard stood up and told me I had to jump or go back down the stairs—all five hundred of them. But if I did that, Miles would never stop making fun of me. And so I just stood there—paralyzed.

"And then, up there on the high dive, I felt an arm around my shoulder. It was Miles. He'd cut ahead of the long line and climbed the stairs to help me out of my terrible predicament.

"'It's okay, Caree,' he said. 'I'll jump with you.'

"I looked at him like he was crazy.

"He said, 'Really. It's okay. We'll jump at the same time so it won't be so scary for you.'

"I looked at him and nodded my head, 'Okay'—I couldn't have made a sound if my life depended on it.

"And then he said, 'I'll count to three and we'll jump together. I'll go off to the right and you go off to the left.' I nodded my head one more time . . . and then we jumped.

"That day stands out in my mind as a time when I absolutely knew my little brother loved me, and he'd be there to take care of me. He helped me overcome a fear that day—a fear of heights but, more importantly, a fear of taking risks.

"Perhaps you've heard that Miles had a kind of religious conversion during the last few weeks of his life. It's true—although he would've found other words to describe what took place. Over the years, he and I had lots of . . . lively discussions . . . about God. We both grew up with some religious experiences . . . but they weren't all good. So when both of us went away to college, we went away from faith as well. A few years later, though, I found a faith that saw science and Christianity as complements not competition. Miles and I talked about that a lot.

"For a long time he thought I was crazy. But I've come to understand that even when it seemed he was dismissing what I said, he really was listening. Good scientists start out with skepticism. And like a good scientist, Miles was taking in all the data, testing all the hypotheses. During all our discussions, he tried to stay objective.

"One day I said to him, 'Miles, I study the physical world—I focus on balance, and what I find most impressive about Christianity is its balance. There's the balance between how sinful I am and how forgiving God is—although those two certainly aren't equivalent. There's the balance between my repentance and God's acceptance. And there's a balance between my longing for eternity and God's fulfilling that longing. When I put my trust in Christ, I find a kind of spiritual balance that has eluded me all my life.'

"I don't know if that makes sense to you, but sometime during this past month it made sense to Miles. He loved to read, and when he read the Bible, especially the gospel of Mark, it all clicked for him. He told me his favorite guy in the Bible was the man who told Jesus, 'I do believe. Help me in my unbelief.'

"About three weeks ago, he told me he needed to stop being so self-reliant and put his trust in what Christ did for him on the cross.

"Some of the last words he said to me were, 'I can't weigh all the evidence forever. I have to reach a conclusion.' He asked me if it was too late for him to become a Christian, and I could tell he was for real. I told him, 'No, Miles, it isn't too late.' I want to say the same thing to each of you as well. And if Miles were here, I think he'd want you to take that leap—jump off the diving board of indecision—and he'd jump with you.

"As I step down now from this podium, my niece Sandra is going to perform a piece that Miles loved to hear her play. It's Ravel's *Pavane pour une infante défunte*. Literally, the title means a 'pavane [or dance] for a dead princess.' But Ravel pointed out another translation of those same words—a 'pavane for a dancing maiden.' This translation defines the piece in a more upbeat way—a more life-filled way. I think that's how Miles would like you to think of him—not as someone who is now dead, but as someone who has found life—eternal life. As you listen to the music, perhaps you'll want to say yes to this kind of life. If you're not ready to do that, perhaps you'll want to say something like, 'I do believe. Help me in my unbelief.'

"Thank you for coming today. May God bless you."

❖

Keep the Conversation Going

- The gospel of Mark could tie together many of the issues raised in this book.
- A very helpful and inspiring book is Joni Eareckson Tada, *Heaven* (Grand Rapids: Zondervan, 1997).

Your Next Conversation

WE FILL OUR DAYS WITH CONVERSATIONS. When not exchanging points with others, we make proclamations inside our own heads—whether we realize it or not. All day long we interact with someone's message—a friend's, a coworker's, a lyric from a song, an image from TV, or some unchallenged belief that resonates below the surface.

Perhaps, as you've eavesdropped on the dialogues in Turnerville, you've had some conversations with yourself. Did you find yourself agreeing with Caryn, that our world shows evidence of a designer? Or do you lean towards Michael's explanation for the problems in the world—"'stuff' happens"? Do you find comfort from Janet's view that, despite the unanswered questions, we can trust a God who has done something about evil? Or do you, like Cathy, feel a sense of despair when faced with pain and tragedy?

Which professor's lectures would you rather hear, Dr. Hart's or Dr. Young's? In other words, do you think the Bible could be helpful to you as you sort out the questions of morality and values? Is it possible that the ancient wisdom from Genesis, Proverbs, and the Gospels might help you the way it helped Dana? Many sincere questioners throughout the centuries have found it worth the effort to investigate.

With whom will you converse next? Perhaps you'll want to hear from one of the authors recommended in the "Keep the Conversation Going" sections. I can tell you that reading the works of C. S. Lewis, John Stott, or any of the others would prove worthwhile.

Maybe you'll dialogue next with the friend who gave you this book. Some ongoing conversations with people of faith, at a church or some kind of fellowship group, could help you connect with God in a personal, conversational way. It could also open up the reality that faith is best experienced in community.

Most significantly, you might feel ready for a conversation with God—the God that some of the people in Turnerville talked about. This might seem awkward at first but many have found this to be a beautiful language to learn— especially people like Kim, who longed for forgiveness, or Miles, who needed assurance of life after death.

If the following prayer expresses what you're sensing inside, why not tell God something like this:

> God, I realize you're more holy and loving than I had imagined. I also acknowledge I'm more sinful and rebellious than I ever admitted. Whatever good things I see in me are gifts from you. Whatever longings I find can only be satisfied in you. I confess I have no quality, no ability, and no accomplishment that could reconcile my sinfulness with your holiness. And so I turn from myself to Jesus and place my trust in what he did on the cross to reunite me with you, my Creator and my Redeemer.

If you've expressed this to God, be sure to tell someone else as well. It will launch a lifetime of conversations you won't want to miss.

How should we share the Good News?

"Ask a question," says Randy Newman. It is, after all, what Jesus did. This "questioning" style of evangelism is without formulas or answers to memorize, and you don't have to have a Ph.D. in theology to use it. If it sounds too simple, don't worry. It worked for Jesus; it will work for you.

0-8254-3324-X • 272 pages

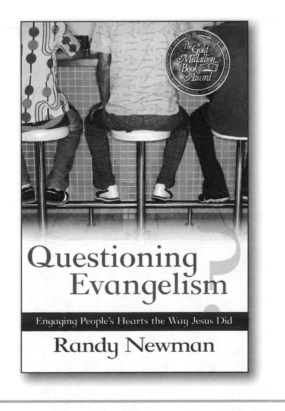